Birds of the Serengeti

and Ngorongoro Conservation Area

Adam Scott Kennedy

PRINCETON
press.princeton.edu

Published by Princeton University Press,
41 William Street, Princeton, New Jersey 08540
In the United Kingdom: Princeton University Press, 6 Oxford Street,
Woodstock, Oxfordshire OX20 1TW
nathist.press.princeton.edu

Requests for permission to reproduce material from this work should be sent to
Permissions, Princeton University Press

British Library Cataloging-in-Publication Data is available

Library of Congress Control Number 2013950254
ISBN 978-0-691-15910-2

Production and design by **WILD**_Guides_ Ltd., Old Basing, Hampshire UK.
Printed in Singapore

10 9 8 7 6 5 4 3 2 1

This book is dedicated to my beautiful
God-daughter, Elvi Wren Clay, who is
destined to become a fabulous naturalist.

Contents

BIRDS OF THE PLAINS

BIRDS OF MARSH AND WATER

BIRDS OF WOODLAND, SCRUB & GARDEN

A view over the Ngorongoro Crater. The forest here supports many wonderful birds.

About this book

The Serengeti is world-famous for the spectacular Wildebeest migration and the predators that prey on them but few visitors anticipate the incredible birdlife that the National Park has to offer. Well over 500 species have been recorded within the park's boundaries and many more in the neighbouring Ngorongoro Conservation Area (NCA). Although several books cover the birdlife of the East African region, until now there has been no dedicated field guide to the birds of the most visited National Park in Tanzania. It therefore gives me great pleasure to introduce 264 of the species most likely to be encountered on a safari to the Serengeti and surrounding area.

To the uninitiated, identifying birds can be a bit of a nightmare but becoming a confident and competent birdwatcher, or birder, is no different from becoming a good soccer player, gardener or writer – it just takes time and practice. Since my first birding trips at the age of four (you can never start too young!) I have found that watching birds with more experienced people is by far the best way to learn and I very much hope that by writing this guide I will be able to help you get the most from your journey, or safari as we say in East Africa.

I shall never forget the time, while on a game-drive with a small group in southern Tanzania, that our guide called a Heuglin's Courser a Harlequin Quail – two species that really shouldn't be confused. As it happens, I was fortunate enough to work closely with that particular guide for several months afterwards and his abiliy to soak up all the bird-related information I could share with him was quite remarkable. In return, he was keen to share with me the reasons why he had struggled to identify birds using the standard field guides to the region: he was unable to relate the illustrations to real birds and did not understand the technical language used in the text. As a direct result of my conversations with this guide, I decided to produce this bird guide, and others in the Wildlife Explorer series, based on high-quality photographic images, and to avoid OTJ – ornithological techno-jargon – at all costs.

Heuglin's Courser

Harlequin Quail
(female)

My wife Vicki was not a birder when I met her and, in polite company at least, will not confess to being one now. But her interest in birds has grown and she is now quite capable of identifying most of the species illustrated in this book. However, the minute I start pointing out greyish supercilia, spotted median coverts and ochre rectrices (all classic OTJ), she switches off. I firmly believe that it doesn't help to bore or baffle people about birds when they're starting out. My message to the professional guides is this: by all means share the really interesting information and your own personal experiences, but leave the OTJ for those who understand the language. Serious birders may sneer at some of the simple terms I have used, but if Vicki and the uninitiated can understand them, anyone can – and that is what this book is all about. For this reason, I have opted not to include a diagram of the feathers and body parts of a bird (definitely OTJ) as I hope that everyone using this book will know the difference between a head, a wing and a tail.

As you can probably tell by now, I have tried to keep this book as light-hearted as possible and there are several pieces of text that I hope will raise a smile. After all, the life of birds and the people who named them are fascinating and, believe it or not, quite entertaining too!

About the images

In collating the photos for this book, I have tried to capture and include the most suitable images to show the variations in sex, age and plumage throughout the year (for example, breeding and non-breeding plumages), both within and between the species. Where I have failed to capture the bird in a desired plumage or pose, the lovely people at **WILD**Guides have very kindly liaised with Greg & Yvonne Dean and Andy & Gill Swash at WorldWildlifeImages.com and obtained the images required. For that I am very grateful to all concerned, as these photos complement the book beautifully. Thanks also to Vicki for letting me use some of her images, which are wonderful. All the images that were not taken by me are fully credited on *page 212*.

A Little Bee-eater eating a dragonfly.

How to use this book

When it comes to organizing which species follows which, most field guides follow a standard order, or systematic list. For this reason, in Africa at least, the Ostrich comes first and the buntings are last. For seasoned birders, this is great because they can pick up almost any bird guide and know that birds of prey (raptors) are quarter the way through, pigeons are somewhere in the middle, and finches are near the back. For those not so familiar with this order, it may require a dip into the index. But if you are not sure what species you are looking for, only that it is a finch of some kind, that's not much help. So this book, which is aimed at all levels of birding ability, adopts a habitat-based approach. Put simply, first decide where you are watching the bird, and then decide from the offering in that section which species you are most likely to be looking at. If you are out on the plains and you see a streaky lark with chestnut in its wings, check out the *Plains* section and there you will find it – Rufous-naped Lark (*page 63*). If you are in the dry acacia scrub and see a streaky lark, check out the *Acacia Scrub* section and you will find the Foxy Lark (*page 173*). I hope you find this as simple and straightforward as it is intended to be.

Of course, birds are very mobile creatures that move around from one place to another – so there is every chance that you may encounter a species away from its typical habitat. Birds such as swallows and swifts spend much of their lives in the air and may not be restricted to any particular habitat. For that reason, such species have their own 'habitat' – up in the air – but guidance is still given about where you are most likely to find them. Similarly, nocturnal birds hide away very well during the daytime and are most likely to be seen on tracks and roads at night, so a section for nocturnal birds was also required.

The English names used for the birds in this book are those most widely used in Tanzania. As these may differ from the names given in other books, the most frequently used alternative names are also referenced. A list of the universally recognized scientific names for each of the species covered in this book is included on *pages 213–216*. The sizes shown for each bird indicates its length from the tip of the bill to the end of the tail and are given in both centimetres (cm) and inches ("). To help you keep a record of the birds you see, a small tick-box has been included next to each species description.

Ostrich with Thomson's Gazelles

The habitats

Nature does not permit easy categorization, and deciding which species is associated with each habitat is not always simple and straightforward. For example, in the middle of a vast grassy plain you may find a single thick bush with a bird sitting on top. Which habitat section of this book would you open to find and identify your mystery bird? The best place to start would be the **Plains** section – but if that fails try the **Open woodland, bush and garden** section. However, if your bird has long legs and a strong bill that might be used for fishing, then maybe it is a species of heron that has made a quick pit-stop before flying on to the nearest marsh. In this case, you should find it in the **Marsh and water** section.

The habitat sections in this book have been colour-coded, as summarized in the box above, in an attempt to make the process of finding your bird as simple as possible.

Plains	*24–71*
Marsh and water	*72–103*
Woodland, scrub and garden	*104–165*
Acacia scrub	*166–177*
Village	*178–181*
Forest	*182–185*
Birds of the air	*186–185*
Nightbirds	*196–199*
Lake Victoria specials	*200–209*

Plains

The grassy plains covering the majority of the Serengeti and Ngorongoro Conservation Area (NCA) can be divided into two main types: short and long.

The short grass plains are continually grazed by the game and, in the conservancy lands, also by domestic animals. They provide limited protection for the birds that live there but do allow these species to see danger coming from afar. Common species include various plovers and the smart **Temminck's Courser** (*page 31*).

The long grass plains consist of grass species that are not particularly palatable to grazing animals. These areas afford protective cover for ground-nesting birds such as the various **bustards**, **longclaws** and **larks**. Other species, including the **Buffy Pipit** (*page 69*), prefer to feed on the open short grass plain but nest in the longer grass.

The plains are typically characterized by a variety of grasses and low shrubs, with occasional trees.

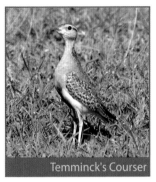
Temminck's Courser

Kori Bustard

13

Marsh and water

Pages 72–103

The Grumeti River is the most significant water body in the National Park but various smaller rivers (*e.g.* Mbalageti) also flow through it and there are also some impressive marshes (*e.g.* Olbalbal).

There are also some impressive lakes in the NCA (*e.g.* Magadi and Masek), where gatherings of flamingos, waterfowl and shorebirds can be spectacular at certain times of year.

After any substantial rainfall, many of the grassland areas of the reserve become waterlogged and afford feeding grounds for a number of typically wetland bird species such as **Hamerkop** (*page 78*) and **Three-banded Plover** (*page 97*).

Pied Kingfisher

Hamerkop

A feeding flock of Lesser Flamingos on Lake Magadi in the Ngorongoro Crater.

Woodland, scrub & garden

Pages 104–165

Many camps and lodges are located amongst tall trees that afford some protection from the sun's heat during the middle of the day. Camps such as Grumeti River Camp are situated in riverine (or riparian) woodland, while others such as Serengeti Serena have a different array of tree species in their impressive gardens.

Several lodges, such as the decadent Ngorongoro Crater Lodge, even have wonderfully manicured gardens with exuberant flowers and lawns, all of which offer superb feeding and breeding sites for a wide array of species that may be difficult to see elsewhere. An early morning walk with a guide or resident bird enthusiast around the camp or lodge where you are staying is highly recommended as a great way to connect with a good variety of African garden birds. Aim to start between 6 am and 7 am to get the most from your experience.

Fischer's Lovebirds

Variable Sunbird

Hotel and lodge grounds can be very rewarding for birding.

Acacia scrub

A quintessentially African tree family, acacias are a varied mix of hardy trees and bushes that support a unique selection of birds. Although you may see scattered acacias almost anywhere in the National Park, the best acacia scrub habitats are found in the south and east of the park and within the Ngorongoro Conservation Area (NCA) .

Many of the acacia-dwelling species, such as **Silverbird** (*page 172*) and **Abyssinian Scimitarbill** (*page 168*) cover vast areas in a day, so expect to spend some time searching for them.

Silverbird

Whistling Thorn dominates large areas of the Western Corridor and the NCA.

Village

As with every other human habitation around the world, the towns, villages and Maasai *bomas* around the reserve are home to some resourceful species that have adapted successfully to a world created by people.

Crows and several species of **sparrow** and **finch** are most easily found around these places and many will be common close to some larger camps and lodges too.

Pied Crow

A typical Maasai village in the Ngorongoro Conservation Area.

Red-billed Firefinch

Forest

The mature forests surrounding the rims of the numerous volcanic craters of the Ngorongoro Conservation Area (NCA) support a number of special birds that are rarely found elsewhere. In particular, the huge fruiting fig trees are the main attraction to a number of fruit-eating birds such as **hornbills** and **turacos**.

Crowned Hornbill

Schalow's Turaco

Up in the air

A flock of Little Swifts

Many birds can be seen flying from one place to another but there are two families of bird that spend most of their lives 'up in the air': the **swallows and martins** (*pages 186–191*) and the **swifts** (*pages 192–193*). Because they can cover such large areas in the course of the day, these birds are likely to be encountered over many different habitats – but their true habitat is the sky where they feed and, in the case of swifts, even mate on the wing.

Night birds

Owls and **nightjars** are birds of the night and although you may be fortunate enough to see them during the day, usually roosting, your best chance of an encounter is during a night-drive.

If you are staying within the National Park boundary, do check with your accommodation about the possibility of night-drives although typically they are not permitted. However, if you are staying in one of the surrounding conservancies then a night-drive may be permitted and is highly recommended for nocturnal birds and some rarely seen mammals.

Verreaux's Eagle Owl

The Square-tailed or Gabon Nightjar is frequently encountered on roads and tracks at night.

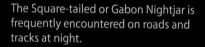

Lake Victoria specials

Pages 200–209

Situated just a few kilometres from the western Ndabaka Gate of the Serengeti are the sandy shores of Lake Victoria and the calming waters of the Speke Gulf.

On a good day, you could be forgiven for thinking you have just been transported to a "tropical island", such is the tranquillity of the area, but better still there are lots of new birds to be found here that are unlikely to be encountered even in the nearby Serengeti.

The bird-rich gardens of Speke Bay Lodge are where I photographed many of the images presented here and they also have a resident bird guide offering walks and advice.

The reedy margins of Lake Victoria are home to many of the species shown on *pages 200–209*.

Yellow-backed Weaver

White-winged Black Tern

Map of the 'Greater Serengeti area'
showing locations mentioned in the text

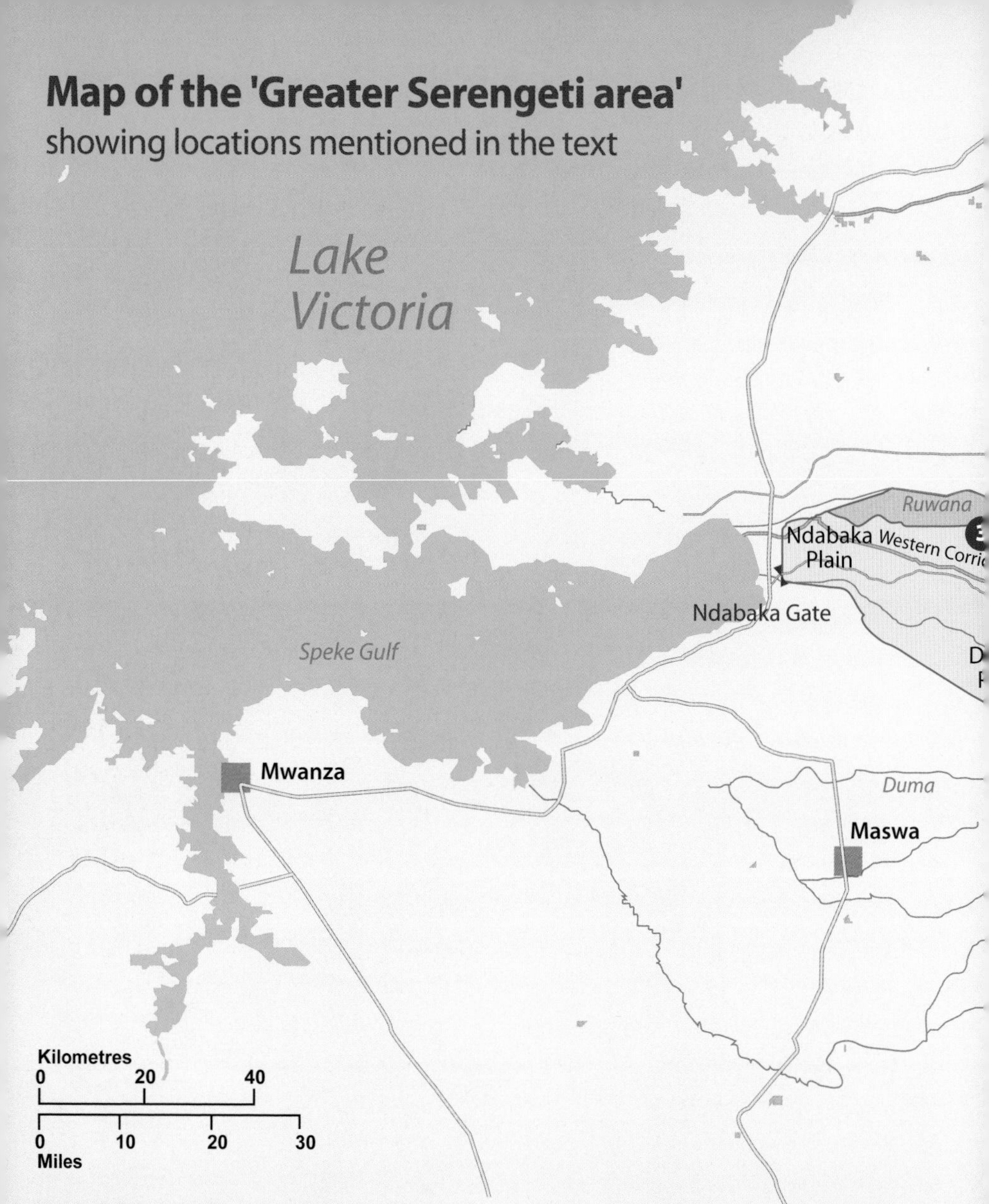

Lake Victoria

Ruwana

Ndabaka Plain

3

Western Corridor

Ndabaka Gate

Speke Gulf

D P

Mwanza

Duma

Maswa

Kilometres
0   20   40

0   10   20   30
Miles

Key wildlife watching locations

1 Ngorongoro Crater

2 Seronera Valley

3 The Western Corridor

4 Olmoti and Empakaai Craters

5 Moru Kopjes

6 Ndutu Plains

7 Olduvai Gorge

8 Angata Kiti and Gol Mountains

9 Grumeti River

10 Lobo Valley

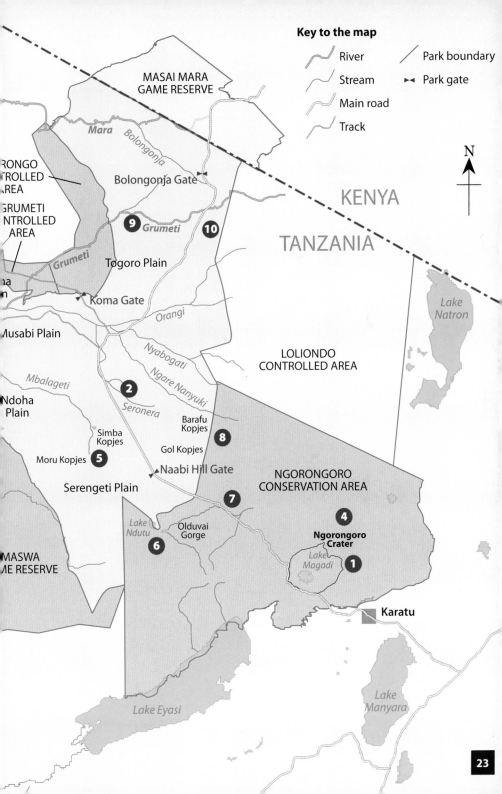

Key to the map

River		Park boundary
Stream		►◄ Park gate
Main road		
Track		

MASAI MARA
GAME RESERVE

KENYA

TANZANIA

N

Mara

Bolongonja

RONGO
TROLLED
REA

Bolongonja Gate

GRUMETI
NTROLLED
AREA

9 *Grumeti*

10

Grumeti

Tøgoro Plain

Koma Gate

Orangi

Lake
Natron

Musabi Plain

Nyabogati

LOLIONDO
CONTROLLED AREA

Mbalageti

Ngare Nanyuki

2

Seronera

Ndoha
Plain

Barafu
Kopjes

Simba
Kopjes

8

Moru Kopjes **5**

Gol Kopjes

NGORONGORO
CONSERVATION AREA

Naabi Hill Gate

Serengeti Plain

7

4

Lake
Ndutu

Olduvai
Gorge

**Ngorongoro
Crater**

6

*Lake
Magadi*

1

MASWA
ME RESERVE

Karatu

Lake Eyasi

Lake
Manyara

Male

◼ **Ostrich** 250 cm | 98"

Huge, unmistakable birds. Males are distinguished by their black body feathers, white wing plumes and short, white tail. The pink skin of the head, neck and long, strong legs becomes flushed when birds are excited. This is particularly so during display, which involves exuberant rolling and shaking of the wing plumes. Females and immature birds are greyish-brown in colour and lack pink tones to the skin. Eggs are laid in a scrape in the ground that several females may share. The call is a deep "*hoo-hoo-whoooooo*" that sounds similar to a Lion's roar from a distance.

RECORD BREAKER

This is the largest bird in the world, lays the largest and heaviest eggs, and is the only flightless bird of mainland Africa. Although it is the only bird in the world with two toes on each foot, the Ostrich is capable of sprints in excess of 60 kph, making it the fastest running of all birds.

Female

Chicks are able to walk within minutes of hatching. They have a number of dark stripes down their rusty-coloured head and neck.

25

☐ Secretarybird 140 cm | 55" ▼

A tall and elegant bird often seen walking through long grass in search of prey. Even from a considerable distance, the light-grey plumage with black flight feathers and knee-length 'trousers' is distinctive. The attractive face of bare, red skin is decorative, and there are black plumes at the back of the head. The sexes are alike. Immature birds are browner all-over with yellowish facial skin. The legs are long and pink and the toes are short. These it uses to club and tackle dangerous snakes, such as puff adder and cobra, although they will also take other reptiles, small birds and mammals. Birds typically roost on top of a solitary tree or bush, and it is in such places that they usually build their nest. In flight, the long, black-tipped, grey tail is conspicuous and it also shows a white rump. It is generally silent but sometimes growls, especially at the nest.

Although the head plumes may resemble a secretary's quill, the bird's name is actually a corruption of *saqr-et-tair*, a word derived from Arabic meaning hunter-bird.

▼ ☐ Grey Crowned Crane 110 cm 43"

Very attractive birds of open plains and marshes. The crown of fine, golden feathers sits on a black, velvety forehead, and below the clean white face disc hangs a red wattle. Although sometimes seen in large flocks, especially within the Ngorongoro Crater, these birds are more often encountered in pairs walking sedately and feeding by pecking at seeds. If very lucky, you may see them break into a joyous, hopping display dance, which is one of the finest sights of the Serengeti and NCA. Pairs build a floating nest in a shallow pool. The chicks are yellow and rather cute, though immature birds are quite scruffy. The call is a loud honking "*hu-wonk*" that is often given in flight, when they also show large white patches on the forewing.

This is the national bird of Uganda, and is 'Grey' and 'Crowned' rather than 'Grey-crowned'. The distinction is made because there is also a Black Crowned Crane found in West Africa.

Black-bellied Bustard

White-bellied Bustard

☐ **Kori Bustard** 128 cm | 50" ▼

A very large, thickset bird of open areas that often seeks shade under a tall tree. Males are considerably larger than females but the sexes are otherwise similar. The face, neck and breast are lightly barred with grey, the crown is black and there is a black stripe running through the eye. The back and flight feathers are greyish-brown and the upperwing is peppered with black and white markings. During their display (see *page 212*), which can be seen from a great distance, male birds will stand and strut with raised crest, the neck feathers puffed up into a large white balloon, and the tail brought up and over the back. The call is a deep repeated "*woomp*" given when in display.

RECORD BREAKER
The Kori Bustard can leap into flight from a standing start and is the heaviest of all flying birds, reaching 42 lb (19 kg).

Black-bellied Bustard 64 cm | 25"

A small bustard of long grass plains. During the breeding season (March to May), males perform an amazing display, usually from raised ground such as a grassy knoll. They stand with their neck raised then throw back their head abruptly making a "*kwaark*" sound. With the neck coiled back, the bird then growls softly before letting out the air in a belched "*pop!*" about five seconds after the initial recoil. On a quiet day, it is possible to hear other males making the same display call just a short distance away. Adult birds look spectacular in flight and show a strongly contrasting black-and-white wing pattern which is obvious from many kilometres away, especially as the males make exaggerated wing flaps during aerial circuits of their territories.

White-bellied Bustard 61 cm | 24"

A small, pale bustard of short grass areas, often with scattered small trees and shrubs. The black-and-white face markings of the male, finished with red 'lipstick' on the bill, are distinctive. When displaying to females, they walk with their neck outstretched and their black throat inflated. Females are similar to the female Black-bellied Bustard but can be easily separated by their stronger face markings and soft-blue colouration to the back of the neck. In flight, this species does not show any white in the wing. However, as with all bustards, it is reluctant to fly, preferring instead to walk away from danger.

Female

Male

Female

Male

☐ Double-banded Courser 24 cm | 9¼"

A small, well-camouflaged wader of the short grass plains and open scrub. The scaled pattern on the back of this bird makes it almost impossible to find when it is facing away from you, especially on stony ground. But it is much easier to find when it is front-on and the two distinctive black bands can be seen clearly. It tends to stand upright and remains still when approached, eventually running and taking off when danger gets too close. Unlike Temminck's Courser, the underwing is pale in flight. As is typical of small birds that live in open areas, the eggs and young are very well camouflaged.

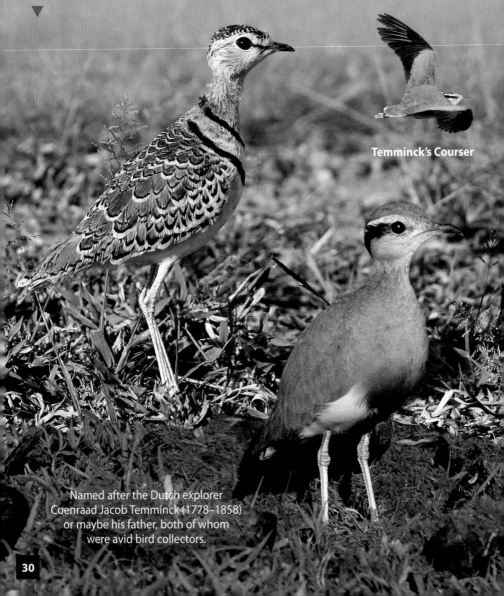

Temminck's Courser

Named after the Dutch explorer Coenraad Jacob Temminck (1778–1858) or maybe his father, both of whom were avid bird collectors.

☐ Temminck's Courser
21 cm | 8¼"

Small, erect-standing birds of the short grass plains. Usually found in pairs or small parties in very open areas, where they habitually run, stop and then peck at an item on the ground – often a small grub or other invertebrate. It is quite common to find them rummaging through a small dung pile, where various food items can be found. They are reluctant to fly, preferring to run from any threat, but when they do take flight they show a short tail, beyond which the long legs project, and very rounded wings that are entirely black underneath, creating a distinctive silhouette. Immature birds (*page 13*) show heavily marked wings, suggesting Double-banded Courser but head pattern and belly patch are useful identification features. Of the four species of courser recorded in the Serengeti, Temminck's is the most often seen, as it is both fairly common and has far less cryptic plumage than either Double-banded or Heuglin's Courser (*page 107*).

Named in honour of Friedrich Heinrich Freiherr von Kittlitz (1799-1874), who was not only a great ornithologist and explorer but also a fabulous artist and a naval officer. In addition to travels around North Africa, he also studied the Pacific Rim on a round-the-world journey.

▼ ☐ Kittlitz's Plover 15 cm | 6"
A small, attractive wader of short-grass plains and shorelines. Unlike the similar small plovers included in this book (*pages 97 & 209*), Kittlitz's Plover does not have a breast-band but does show a black stripe running through the face. The forehead and throat are white and the underparts are buffy-brown in colour. This plover leads a double life, spending the breeding season on short-grass plains and much of the year residing close to edges of lakes.

Large plovers within the scientific genus *Vanellus*, including those on this and the opposite page, and on *pages 92–93*, are also known as lapwings.

☐ Crowned Plover 31 cm | 12¼" ▼

A common and distinctive wader of the open plains. This species is slightly larger than the Black-winged Plover and has longer, bright-pink legs. It is best identified by the characteristic head pattern (a black-and white skullcap) from which it derives its name. This species also shows a unique wing pattern which makes it easy to separate from other large plovers, either in flight or when wing-stretching – something it often does when a vehicle approaches close-by. These birds draw a great deal of attention to themselves when performing noisy intimidation flights aimed at distracting predators, such as jackals, birds of prey and Southern Ground Hornbills from their eggs or chicks. If the predator persists, the plovers will often resort to dive-bombing their enemies which can bring them perilously close to danger – so it is always worth watching to see who wins.

Spur-winged Plover
(*page 93*)

Crowned Plover

Black-winged Plover

Senegal Plover

◻ Senegal Plover 26 cm | 10"

A slim and long-legged wader of grassy plains and open woodland. This elegant bird is easily confused with the similar Black-winged Plover but always appears more dainty and elongated than that species. Its legs are long and extend much further beyond the tail in flight than in Black-winged Plover, but it is the distinctive wing patterns of these two species that are the best identification feature: Senegal Plover shows a triangle of white on the trailing edge of the wing, whereas Black-winged Plover has a solid white band across the wing. Another useful identification feature is the white spot above the bill that is crisp and shows more contrast with the darker head than on Black-winged Plover. These waders move with the rains and will also gather in large numbers on recently burned ground to feast on invertebrates. ▼

◻ Black-winged Plover
27 cm | 10½"

Chunky waders of open grassy plains. Similar in shape and build to other large plovers but shows a clear black band across the breast, a feature only shared with the slimmer Senegal Plover which can also be separated in flight by the distinctive wing patterns. They are mostly blue-grey in the face and usually show a white patch above the bill, although this is less obvious in females. Black-winged Plovers are often found in loose flocks of up to 20 birds but during September to November they congregate in larger flocks. Their distinctive "*chi-chi-chi chireeek*" call can often be heard at night. ▼

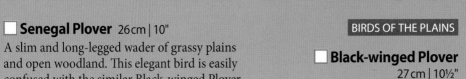

☐ Black-faced Sandgrouse 23 cm | 9" ▶

A small, plump sandgrouse of dry, open areas. Although it feeds on a diet of seeds, this sandgrouse is less restricted to short grass than the larger Yellow-throated Sandgrouse and may also be found in dry thorny scrub where it can be difficult to locate. Only males show the distinctive black face but both sexes have a white breast-band. In flight, both sexes appear dark-bellied and the blackish flight feathers contrast strongly with the rest of the wing, which is pale. This species is more strict than other sandgrouse in its habit of drinking at waterholes only twice per day and usually when it is dark.

☐ Yellow-throated Sandgrouse 31 cm | 12"

A gregarious, stocky bird of the very short grass plains. In their rapid, direct flight these birds can be mistaken for overweight pigeons, whereas on the ground they behave like short-legged gamebirds and are usually found in loose flocks that may exceed 50 birds. Their diet of grass seeds is especially dry, so flocks routinely seek water twice a day – at first light and again late in the afternoon – preferring shallow, open puddles, but they may also be seen drinking at other times of day. Male birds look very smart with their yellow throats bordered with a black chinstrap, while females are suitably camouflaged for incubation duties. Listen out for the charming call, a gargled "*a-coocoowoowoo*".

☐ Chestnut-bellied Sandgrouse 28 cm | 11" ▼

A plain-faced sandgrouse with a long, pointed tail. This medium-sized sandgrouse is common throughout the NCA and eastern Serengeti, typically in dry, stony areas. Males show a single thin black line across the lower breast and a rich-chestnut coloured belly that may appear black in strong light. Females may be confused with female Black-faced Sandgrouse but the long tail feathers always project well beyond the closed wing. In flight, the underwing and belly appear uniformly dark and this is the only sandgrouse that shows a neat white line along the rear edge of the open wing.

Female

Male

In the breeding season, males soak their absorbent belly feathers in water and return to the nest where the chicks can then draw the moisture.

Female

Male

Male

Female

White Stork 122 cm | 48" ▼

Distinctive mostly-white storks of long grass plains. These birds are non-breeding migrants from Europe that usually arrive on the northern plains during October and leave in late April, although a few birds have been known to stay in southern Africa to breed. They frequently gather in vast flocks numbering in excess of 5,000 birds that move, according to the rains, around the Serengeti where they can be seen feeding alongside the hordes of Wildebeest. The only other 'white' stork with which this bird could be confused is the Yellow-billed Stork (*page 75*), but the longer, yellow bill and red facial skin of that species are distinctive. In Europe, White Storks are frequently found nesting on the rooftops of buildings and feature in traditional European folklore as the deliverer of babies.

As with all storks, the White Stork has no syrinx, or vocal cord, which prohibits them from making any calls. Instead, you may sometimes hear them clatter their bills.

Abdim's Stork 81 cm | 32" ▼

A mostly black stork with a colourful face. Like the White Stork, the Abdim's Stork is a non-breeding migrant that can often be seen in huge numbers in the Serengeti and NCA. However, this bird is a migrant that breeds in central Africa where it is considered a good luck symbol and bringer of the rains. Like other grassland storks, this bird walks endlessly in search of grasshoppers, locusts, small reptiles and amphibians. Abdim's is the smallest of all true storks and shows a white belly in flight and a conspicuous white rump that is best seen from above. This separates it from the rarely encountered Black Stork (*not shown*), another migrant from Europe, that has a black rump.

Named after the Governor of Wadi Halfa, Ben El-Arnaut Abdim, a Turkish civil servant working in Sudan from 1821 to 1827, who assisted Rüppell (of Rüppell's Vulture fame, *page 39*) during his collecting expeditions in North Africa.

Southern Ground Hornbill
102 cm | 40"

Huge, black, turkey-like terrestrial birds of the open plains. Usually encountered in family groups that may include immature birds and mature offspring of previous broods. Adults of both sexes show red facial skin and a saggy wattle, but the female can be separated by the small patch of violet-blue colour on the throat. Look out for the incredibly long eyelashes on this bird. They are reluctant fliers and prefer to hop and run away from danger but they will always fly to roost in trees at dusk when they reveal clean white outer flight feathers. Listen out for their wonderful calls, usually at dawn, a deep, booming "*ooomp-ooomp-wa-woomp*" that carries for many ▼ kilometres.

These huge birds can walk for over 30 km a day in search of invertebrates, reptiles and young birds.

☐ **Marabou Stork** 152cm | 60"

A huge, ugly stork. This bird is a regular scavenger at the carcass where it uses its enormous bill to great effect. It will often wait for the more aggressive vultures to have their fill before stepping in to clean up the scraps. The head is mostly featherless, enabling it to get deep into the carcass without getting blood over its plumage; bare skin being easier to keep clean than feathers. Marabous often congregate along the Grumeti and Mara Rivers when the Wildebeest migration passes through where gatherings feast on the many carcasses that litter the channels. Unlike other storks that fly with their necks outstretched, the Marabou carries its head close to its body like a heron.

RECORD BREAKER
Some large individuals have a wingspan in excess of 3·5m (10 feet), making this species, together with the Andean Condor of South America, the longest-winged of all land birds.

In many parts of Africa, the Marabou is known as the 'undertaker' on account of its habit of opening its wings over a carcass as though it is measuring it up for a coffin!

See *pages 42–43* for vultures in flight

☐ Rüppell's Vulture 104 cm | 41"

A larger vulture than the similar White-backed Vulture, Rüppell's is reliably told from that species by its cream-coloured bill. Adult birds also show obvious pale scalloping to the wing feathers and never a white rump in flight. The movements of Rüppell's Vulture tend to follow closely the movements of the Wildebeest migration but birds can be found in the Serengeti year-round, even when the migration crosses the border into the Masai Mara. It nests on remote, precipitous cliffs and therefore has to fly farther than the resident White-backed Vultures to feed. Being larger than the White-backed, it can easily use its strength to out-compete that species when similar numbers are present at the carcass, but it is rarely the first to arrive. ▼

This bird is named after the German Wilheim Rüppell (1794–1884) whose zoological and ethnographical collections from North Africa dated between 1822 and 1833.

☐ White-backed Vulture 98 cm | 39"

The commonest vulture in the Serengeti-Mara ecosystem. At first glance, many vulture species may appear quite similar but it pays to know 'who is who' when watching these birds at the carcass, as the different species have different feeding behaviours and strategies. White-backs play the 'numbers game', benefitting most when ten or more of its kind are at a carcass. With such numbers it may use intimidation tactics to push other, larger species away. It can be identified by the all-black bill (compare with Rüppell's Vulture) and the plain-brown plumage on the wings. Adult birds appear very pale, almost white, especially in flight when the belly and underwing contrast with the dark flight feathers. The white rump can only be seen from above and rarely when the bird is on the ground. Immature birds are mostly brown all-over, including the rump, but share the black bill of the adult. It is a regular breeder in the area, preferring to nest in trees, and affords some level of protection to other birds, such as starlings and weavers, that are nesting in the same tree. ▼

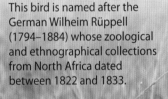

☐ White-headed Vulture 84 cm | 33"

An attractive-looking vulture with a pale head. This bird is the anomaly among vultures in that it rarely attends a large carcass. Instead, it prefers to seek out its own smaller prey items, although it will sometimes scavenge from a recent Bateleur or Tawny Eagle kill. Immature birds, which lack the crisp white head feathers of the adults, may struggle to find their own prey once they leave the nest and are more likely to visit a large carcass. However, because its strategy is simply to wait until the other large vultures have had their fill, it is often the last to feed alongside the smaller but more numerous Hooded Vultures. For this reason, White-headed Vultures are most likely to be encountered in flight, as they typically spend more hours searching for their prey. Adults of both sexes have a white belly and females have white in the flight feathers closest to the body. Immature birds in flight appear very dark, apart from the head, and may show a narrow white line cutting across the underwing from body to wing-tip. Just a few pairs nest in the Serengeti and NCA.

☐ Hooded Vulture 75 cm | 30"

A small vulture with a bare, pink head. Generally found in small groups, the Hooded Vulture is usually seen at the periphery of the carcass waiting for the other, larger vultures to have their fill. Its bill is especially slim for a vulture as it does not need to rip open any skin or flesh; that work has already been done by the time it gets a chance to feed. Instead, it has the perfect tool for tearing at the smaller tendons and scraps often deep inside the remains of the carcass. Adult birds have a pink, bare-skinned face often topped with a white 'woolly wig'. Immature birds show darker 'woolly' head feathers and blue skin on the face. In flight, it appears all-dark and the tail is short and squared, compared to the wedge-shaped tail of the similar sized but whiter Egyptian Vulture (*page 45*). Like the White-backed (*page 39*) and Lappet-faced Vultures, this bird nests in trees, although few pairs breed locally.

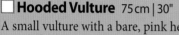

Immature
Hooded Vulture

Immature
White-headed Vulture

Adult
Hooded Vulture

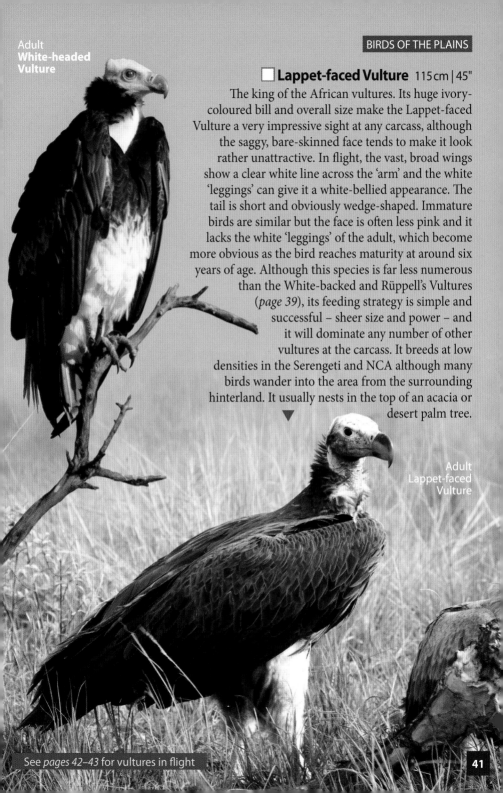

Adult
**White-headed
Vulture**

☐ **Lappet-faced Vulture** 115 cm | 45"

The king of the African vultures. Its huge ivory-coloured bill and overall size make the Lappet-faced Vulture a very impressive sight at any carcass, although the saggy, bare-skinned face tends to make it look rather unattractive. In flight, the vast, broad wings show a clear white line across the 'arm' and the white 'leggings' can give it a white-bellied appearance. The tail is short and obviously wedge-shaped. Immature birds are similar but the face is often less pink and it lacks the white 'leggings' of the adult, which become more obvious as the bird reaches maturity at around six years of age. Although this species is far less numerous than the White-backed and Rüppell's Vultures (*page 39*), its feeding strategy is simple and successful – sheer size and power – and it will dominate any number of other vultures at the carcass. It breeds at low densities in the Serengeti and NCA although many birds wander into the area from the surrounding hinterland. It usually nests in the top of an acacia or desert palm tree.

Adult
Lappet-faced
Vulture

See *pages 42–43* for vultures in flight

☐ **White-headed Vulture** (*page 40*) ▶
Wingspan 215 cm | 85"
The 'easy' one. Extensive white on the belly and, in
females, white inner flight feathers are give-aways.

☐ **Lappet-faced Vulture** (*page 41*) ▼
Wingspan 290 cm | 114"

The 'massive' one. An enormous
bird with baggy white 'shorts' and
an obvious white bar across the
front of the underwing. The large,
pink head is usually visible.

◀ ☐ **Rüppell's Vulture** (*page 39*)
Wingspan 260 cm | 102"

The 'scaly' one. Look out for cream bars
running across the belly and underwing.

☐ **Hooded Vulture** ▶
(*page 40*)
Wingspan 170 cm | 67"

The 'small dark' one
(but still a very large bird).
This is the darkest of the
vultures, although adults
show a silvery sheen to
the base of their flight
feathers.

☐ **Egyptian Vulture** (*page 45*)
Wingspan 165 cm | 65"
The 'black-and-white' one.
Adults are mostly off-white
with solid black flight feathers.
The dark-brown immatures are
similar to Hooded Vulture
but Egyptian always
shows a heavily
wedged tail.
▼

Adult

Adult

Immature

Adult

☐ **White-backed Vulture** (*page 39*) ▲
Wingspan 230 cm | 90"

The 'common' one. Adults have a white underwing contrasting
with the darker flight feathers. Immatures are dark brown under
much of the wing and show a white bar near the front of the wing.

☐ **Martial Eagle** 84 cm | 33"

A massive, powerful eagle of open areas. The dark, greyish-brown head, back and chest of the adult contrasts with the white belly that always shows large, dark spots. Young birds appear very different, having entirely white underparts, a pale head topped with dark flecks, and a cold-looking grey-brown back that appears scaly due to the pale feather edges; features of the adult plumage are gradually acquired over the course of six years. Birds of all ages sport a short, shaggy crest but this is not always obvious. In flight, the underwing appears very dark in adults but pale in young birds (see *page 50*). This species is often seen soaring high in search of prey but will also watch for prey from a perch. It is a ferocious predator that is known to kill baboons, antelope and large birds including storks, guineafowl and even other birds of prey. Martial Eagles usually nest on top of a large tree and, like many other top predators, has a low rate of reproduction, with just one youngster raised every two years.

☐ Black-chested Snake Eagle
68 cm | 27"

A medium-sized, black-and-white eagle of the open plains. It appears similar to the much larger Martial Eagle but adults show a darker head and lack the spots on the belly. In flight (*page 51*), the underwing appears mostly white with three or four narrow black bars running across the flight feathers. Immature birds are mostly brown with a pale face and the underparts are mottled with untidy rufous patches. Snake eagles lack the baggy, feathered thighs of Martial Eagle and show bare, grey legs when perched. It will sometimes use an exposed perch to watch for its next meal – but look out for this bird hovering in search of snakes and other reptiles.

☐ Egyptian Vulture 70 cm | 28"

A stunning white vulture with a yellow face and black flight feathers. Once widespread and common across East Africa, this wonderful vulture has declined drastically in recent decades and is now extremely rare in the region, with only a few pairs remaining in the Serengeti and the surrounding wilderness. As with all other African vulture species, it is an unintended victim of poisoned carcasses that are set as baits for unwanted predators – see recommended reading on *page 210* to find out more about this tragic situation.

It is occasionally seen scavenging at carcasses in the Serengeti but is also able to find its own prey, including Ostrich eggs which it breaks by tossing stones at them! Immature birds are dark sooty-brown and birds of all ages show a distinctive wedge-shaped tail in flight (*page 43*).

Adult

45

See *pages 50–51* for raptors in flight

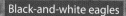

Verreaux's Eagle 96 cm | 38"

A large black eagle of cliffs and gorges. This stunning bird of prey feeds almost exclusively on Rock Hyrax, a guinea-pig sized mammal, which it picks off cliff faces and kopjes after a rapid swoop. However, it may occasionally tackle small monkeys, gamebirds and small antelope. When not engaged in hunting activities, birds spend a great deal of time perched on cliffs and this is when you may see the white braces that roll over the bird's back. The striking white rump is generally only seen with a top view of the bird in flight.

Augur Buzzard 60 cm | 24"

A broad-winged raptor of arid areas. Two distinct colour variations are found in the region, known as light and dark forms, although the light form is by far the most common. Light birds show an all-white throat, breast and belly, whereas dark birds are mostly black all-over. In flight (*page 51*), all birds show white at the base of the flight feathers, and a view of the upperwing reveals a chequered pattern on these same feathers. All adults show a rich-orange tail, although the tail is brown in immature birds. They frequently hover for long periods or just hang in the wind barely moving their wings. This is the only resident buzzard in the Serengeti and is widespread throughout.

46

☐ **Bateleur** 70cm 28" ▶

The classic soaring bird of the open plain. It shows a distinctive silhouette in flight (*page 51*) with swept-back, angular wings and a tail so short that it sometimes appears to have no tail at all. The chunky, black body and chestnut tail of the adult contrasts markedly with the white underwing, which always shows a black edge to the rear (this is narrow in females and broad in males). Females also show a large, grey band in the flight feathers that can be seen on the upperwing in flight and when perched. Both sexes have red legs and a bare, red face, while immatures show blue-green bare parts and a uniform brown plumage. The commonly heard call is a gruff "*yaaargh*", which is often followed by rapid flapping of the wings. Prey items include small mammals, reptiles and birds, and it is also an active scavenger.

Bateleur is the French word for acrobat and was given to the bird on account of its habit of tipping for balance in flight, like a tight-rope walker.

Look out for this bird perched on telegraph poles and roadside posts, when it can be very approachable.

47

Tawny Eagle 74 cm | 29"

The common large, brown eagle of open plains. Tawny Eagles are highly variable in colouration, with some birds being pale-cream and others very dark with rich chestnut tones, but most are a light coffee-brown. When perched they show a bright yellow gape extending from the strong, hooked bill, and well-feathered legs. Immatures tend to be paler and show whitish lines through the wing that are obvious in flight. As with many birds of prey, Tawny Eagles are most often encountered in flight (*page 50*), when they appear large and robust and show mostly dark flight feathers and a dark tail. It is quite common to see these resident eagles in moult, with wing and tail feathers either missing or still growing, which can give them a scruffy-looking appearance. They are very active hunters of small mammals, such as hares, mongooses and dik-diks, as well as gamebirds and large reptiles including monitor lizards. However, this does not put them above scavenging and they will often flush smaller raptors off their kill and attend a carcass with vultures, where their barking or growling calls are most often heard.

Steppe Eagle 80 cm | 31"

This large, brown eagle is a common migrant from Asia. It was once considered to be a race of the Tawny Eagle but is now treated as a full species that can comfortably be identified in the field. Given a good view, the most reliable identification feature in all ages is the long, bright yellow gape that extends from the bill to the back of the eye; in Tawny Eagle the gape stops below the middle of the eye. Immature birds in flight are even easier to identify as they show a bright cream line running through the middle of the underwing (see *page 50*). Adults are usually very dark brown and many show a blonde patch on the back of the head. It is only likely to be encountered between October and April but can occur in a variety of habitats including open savanna.

Black Kite 61 cm | 24"

An all-dark raptor with a distinctive silhouette in flight (*page 51*): the long wings are typically held with a strong angle at the bend, and it usually shows a noticeable fork in its long tail. In both adult and immature birds, much of the plumage is uniform dark brown. It can be told from eagles by the smaller, yellow bill and its slim body when perched. The Black Kite has a wide distribution across Europe, Africa and Asia, and some ornithologists consider our resident birds to be a distinct species, known as Yellow-billed Kite: It is especially common on the slopes of the Ngorongoro Crater.

Dark individual

Pale individual

Adult

Immature

Raptors in flight

Be aware that three other raptor species more usually associated with woodland may also be encountered on the plains (see *page 105*).

■ **Martial Eagle**
(*page 44*)
Wingspan 260 cm | 102"

A massive eagle. Adults show a dark head and underwing, while immatures are mostly pale beneath with light barring on the tail and flight feathers.

Immature

Adult

Immature

Adult

Adult

■ **Steppe Eagle** (*page 48*) Wingspan 210 cm | 84"
Similar to Tawny Eagle but larger. Immatures show a broad pale stripe running through the wing.

■ **Tawny Eagle**
(*page 48*)
Wingspan 190 cm | 75"

A large brown eagle with a broad, rounded tail.

Immature · Adult

☐ Augur Buzzard (*page 46*)
Wingspan 137 cm | 54"

A round-winged raptor with a short, reddish tail. Dark, light and intermediate forms occur.

Pale form · Dark form

☐ Bateleur (*page 47*) Wingspan 175 cm | 69"

The uniquely shaped 'bulging' wings are often swept-back and the red tail is very short. Immatures begin very brown all-over but become increasingly mottled with black as they mature.

☐ Black-chested Snake Eagle ▶
(*page 45*)
Wingspan 175 cm | 69"

Like a small Martial Eagle but much paler underneath and lacks black spots on the belly. The underwing is especially white, with a few narrow bars along the flight feathers only.

◀ ☐ Black Kite (*page 48*)
Wingspan 150 cm | 59"

An all-brown raptor with a distinctive fork in the tail.

☐ Verreaux's Eagle (*page 46*) ▶
Wingspan 220 cm | 88"

A very large and long-tailed eagle that shows large white panels in the wing but is otherwise black. Note the odd shape of the wings with their obvious bulge.

51

All harriers fly
with their wings
held raised in
a shallow 'V'
and sometimes
appear to float
over the ground.

☐ **Pallid Harrier** 46 cm | 18"

Very similar to Montagu's Harrier and even experts struggle to identify
some individuals. Identifying males is straightforward: they are very pale
grey and white, almost ghostly, but show narrow black patches on the
outer wing. Females and immatures are very similar to Montagu's but
the inner flight feathers usually appear blackish in female Pallid Harrier
and there is usually a whitish collar visible between the breast and
the face. Immatures of both species are warm orange below.
Like the Montagu's Harrier, it is a migrant from Asia most likely
to be seen between October and March.

▼

Female
(immature)

Male

Pallid Harrier

Male

Montagu's Harrier

Female

Male

Montagu's Harrier is named after Colonel
George Montagu (1751–1815), a keen British
naturalist and soldier who served in the
American Revolution, and who unfortunately
died of tetanus after stepping on a rusty nail

The Harrier Hawk is commonly known as the Gymnogene in southern Africa.

Montagu's Harrier 46 cm | 18"

A graceful, long-winged bird of open grasslands. The sexes are very different in appearance, with males mostly grey and females streaky brown. Immature birds are similar to females but show a dark face patch and warm-orange colouration to the underparts and underwing. In the buoyant flight, males show black tips to the wing and a narrow black bar along the middle of the upperwing. The brown females show a whitish belly streaked with brown and a clean white rump patch. Females and immatures of this and similar harrier species are commonly known as 'ringtails'. Montagu's Harrier is a long-distance migrant from Europe and Asia and can usually be found between October and April. Birds often gather to roost, particularly on airstrips and open marshes.

African Harrier Hawk 66 cm | 26"

An elegant grey raptor with a bare face. Adult birds are mostly grey with white, finely barred underparts. In flight, the long, black tail shows a single white band and the wings are grey and broad with darker flight feathers. The bare facial skin is yellow but this often flushes to bright pink when the bird becomes excited. Immature birds are mostly brown and nondescript. Food items include palm fruits and a variety of reptiles and young birds. Unique among African raptors, the Harrier Hawk has double-jointed legs which enable it to explore nest holes of birds by rotating the talons all the way around. Look out for it flying along the edge of the plain and resting in exposed trees where weavers are nesting.

☐ **Lanner Falcon** 46 cm | 18"

A large, powerful falcon of open areas.
The broad, pointed wings and chunky
tail are perfectly designed for aerial
combat. Watching a Lanner chase
its prey, usually a bird up to the size
of a small bustard, in mid-air can be
just as exciting as a Cheetah in full
chase. Sometimes they will attempt to
tackle even larger prey, such as small
antelope and monkeys, but this is
quite unusual. They appear very
pale from below and slate-grey
from above. A good view may also
reveal a smart black moustache
and a chestnut patch on the back
of the neck. Immature birds
are much browner and show a
heavily spotted belly and dark
underwing. The Lanner is
usually solitary but sometimes
flies in family groups, when
adults teach young birds the
skills they require.

Female **Common Kestrel** (*page 57*) for comparison with Lanner Falcom

☐ (African) Black-shouldered Kite
35 cm | 14"

A small, pale raptor of open areas, often encountered perched on top of an acacia. It appears white below and pale grey above, with a dark patch on each 'shoulder'. A close view will reveal bright-red eyes. When perched, notice how the long wings extend beyond the very short, white tail. When searching for prey, such as grasshoppers and small reptiles, it will circle an area of grassland and hover frequently, when it could be mistaken for a kestrel (*pages 56–57*) – although these falcons have a much longer tail. It could also be confused with male harriers (*page 52*) but they also have much longer tails and wings. It has recently had a name change to Black-winged Kite, but for ease of reference the old familiar name is used here.

Grey Kestrel 33 cm | 13"

A stocky, all-grey kestrel. Often found perched in a bare tree, especially along rivers, where it watches patiently for a variety of prey, including grasshoppers and termites. Its bare parts are bright yellow and contrast markedly with the slate-grey plumage. In flight, look out for the finely barred tail and the chequered pattern on the flight feathers. It lays its eggs in the old nests of other birds, with a preference for those of the Hamerkop (*page 78*).

▼

Lesser Kestrel 33 cm | 13"

A gregarious falcon that is very similar to Common Kestrel in most plumages. Given a good view, adult male Lesser Kestrel can easily be separated from Common Kestrel by the blue-grey head, the large blue-grey panel that shows in the folded wing and upperwing in flight, and the unspotted brown back. Females are almost identical to female Common Kestrel although, like the male, appear very pale on the underwing and show just a few dark spots, rather than streaking as seen in Common Kestrel. The longer central tail feathers of Lesser Kestrel create a wedge-shaped tail compared to the rounded tail of Common Kestrel. This species is only likely to be encountered between October and March when it gathers in flocks over the plains, especially around the Naabi Hill gate area.

▼

Male

Lesser Kestrel

Common Kestrel

Male

Female

Female

Grey Kestrel

☐ Common Kestrel 33 cm | 13" ▼

A brown-backed falcon with a long tail. Found in singles and groups, these kestrels are frequently seen hovering over the grass in search of small prey before diving steeply onto their quarry. The sexes are fairly similar although males show more grey in the head and tail; young birds are mostly brown. In flight, all birds show a dark band at the end of the tail. Resident birds, sometimes known as 'Rock Kestrels', are supplemented by migratory birds from Europe and Asia between October and April. Birds often come together to roost on the top of an acacia or desert palm tree, when you may hear their excited high-pitched calls "*kee-kee-kee*".

Male

Female

■ **Lilac-breasted Roller** 38 cm | 15"

A spectacular bird with a kaleidoscope of
colours. Among the most popular of all
birds in the Serengeti, this crow-sized jewel
can be found throughout the area and is
often located on a prominent tree branch
over grassland from which it drops onto
its favoured prey of beetles, grasshoppers
and other invertebrates. In flight, it reveals
brilliant-blue feathers in the wings.
These rollers nest in tree holes and are
very territorial, chasing mammals and
other birds, including huge eagles,
away from the nest area. This is when
you are most likely to hear their
throaty "*kerr-kerr-kerr*" call.
Adults are easily told from the
migrant Eurasian Roller by
the long streamers at the
sides of the tail, although
these are lacking in the
duller immature birds.

Rollers get their name from the
exuberant 'rolling' display flights in
which they perform an impressive
'loop-the-loop'.

58

Lilac-breasted Roller

Eurasian Roller

■ **Eurasian Roller** 31 cm | 12¼"
A colourful seasonal migrant to the Serengeti. At first glance this roller appears similar to the resident Lilac-breasted Roller but can quickly be separated by its all-blue head, throat and breast and, in flight, a richer chestnut 'saddle' on the back. The tail is also shorter and lacks the long tail streamers. The Eurasian Roller arrives from Europe during the October–November rains, when the plumage can appear 'washed out' or pale. After heading to southern Africa for several months it returns north again in March and April, when its colours are bright and fresh. Although vocal on their breeding grounds, they are generally silent in Africa.

Red-billed Oxpecker 22 cm | 8¾"

A red-billed 'tick-bird' found on mammals. Both species of oxpecker can be found on a variety of mammal species from which they famously collect ticks and other skin parasites. However, this apparently symbiotic relationship is not always what it seems. For as well as feasting on a variety of skin parasites and, strangely, ear-wax, oxpeckers are very happy to open wounds and drink the blood of the host, especially Hippos, which are frequently scarred and wounded in territorial fights. Although bill colour is the obvious feature used to separate the species, Red-billed Oxpeckers also have a yellow eye-ring and a uniform brown back, rump and tail (Yellow-billed Oxpeckers have an obviously pale rump). ▶

Yellow-billed Oxpecker
20 cm | 8"

A yellow-and-red-billed 'tick-bird' found on mammals. The bill colour and pale rump, which contrasts noticeably with the darker tail and back, separate this species from the similar Red-billed Oxpecker. Both species nest in tree holes, which are occasionally stolen from other birds. Immatures of the two species could be confused, as both have dark bills, but Yellow-billed Oxpeckers always show a pale rump. The sexes look similar in both species. ▼

Wattled Starling 20 cm | 8" ▶

This rather drab grey starling is a seasonal migrant, large flocks arriving from their breeding grounds in the Rift Valley with the annual Wildebeest migration. Although often seen riding the backs of various mammals, they prefer to feed on the invertebrates disturbed by the game rather than directly off the game itself (unlike the oxpeckers). In flight, they are easily identified by their white rumps that contrast with their black flight and tail feathers. A close view will reveal a bright-yellow patch of skin behind the eye – but the saggy black wattles of the breeding males, from which this bird gets its name, are less frequently seen in the Serengeti, where they are non-breeding visitors only.

Elephants are the only large mammals that will not tolerate oxpeckers on their skin, since it is very sensitive to the sharp claws of these birds.

Non-breeding

Breeding

61

Zitting Cisticola
10 cm | 4"

A tiny and heavily streaked warbler of sedge and grassy areas. Unless it is seen well, or heard, it can be tricky to separate from the Pectoral-patch Cisticola but Zitting Cisticola always shows a conspicuous unstreaked rufous rump in flight, rather than the uniform streaked rump of Pectoral-patch Cisticola.
Other subtle differences include blacker streaks on the back and a longer, white-tipped tail. It is mildly less energetic than the smaller Pectoral-patch Cisticola but is frequently seen in its display flight, when it gives the eponymous "*zit-zit-zit*" call.

▼

Pectoral-patch Cisticola
9 cm | 3½"

A tiny darting bird of long grass plains. At only 9 cm from bill to tail, this is the smallest of the grassland birds – but what it lacks in size it makes up for in energy and abundance. Many pairs occupy a square kilometre of grassland and males are often seen displaying by flying at breakneck speed over the grass and shooting up in the air while making sharp "*chit chit*" clicking sounds before dropping down into cover.

Given a good view, look for the dark patches at the side of the chest, brown crown, and long legs if seen on open ground.

▼

Red-capped Lark 15cm | 6"

An attractive small lark with a preference for short grass plains. The rich-rufous cap and chest patches on this bird contrast with the otherwise plain plumage, making it easily separable from the streak-breasted Rufous-naped Lark. Young birds are greyish and heavily peppered with pale feather edges. In flight, the tail appears very dark but shows lighter brown outer tail feathers. The simple call comprises a series of dry "*chirrp*" notes. It is often found in the company of pipits (*page 69*).

▼

Rufous-naped Lark 18cm | 7"

The common, chunky, brown-streaked lark of long grass plains. This drab-looking bird is frequently encountered on drives through the grassy plains when it springs up from tracks and verges, displaying an obvious chestnut wing patch – the only lark in the Serengeti to show this. Sometimes, birds will run in front of vehicles and avoid taking flight. If so, look out for the obvious crest. The song of this bird is the quintessential sound of the grassy plains, a pleasant whistled "*see-seeuu*" which translates usefully to "*hey Joey*". The similar Crested and Red-winged Larks do not occur in the area.

Despite the bird's name, in East Africa this species rarely shows a rufous-coloured nape (*i.e.* the feathers between the crown and the neck).

▼

Male

Female

Male

Female

64

Fischer's Sparrow Lark
11 cm | 4½"

A tiny lark with a distinctive face pattern. This charming little lark is common in open grassland where it often feeds very close to tracks and roads. It has a tendency to fly off at the last minute, usually when you have not even seen it well, but if you drive slowly it may fly just a short distance before dropping again. The males have obvious white cheeks set in a dark head, the crown and neck being chestnut in colour. Females and immatures lack the dark head but show some chestnut markings on the neck and above the eyes. The soft-grey back colour separates this bird from the darker-bellied Chestnut-backed Sparrow Lark (*not shown*), which is a scarce visitor to the Serengeti, preferring areas with red soil.

Anteater Chat

Sooty Chat

Anteater Chat 18 cm | 7"

All-dark perching birds with a white flash in the flight feathers. Anteater Chats are common in the eastern Serengeti and Crater Highlands and are usually encountered in extended family groups. Unlike the Sooty Chat, which is only found in the north-west of the Serengeti, the sexes of this species are similar and easily identified by the extensive white patches in the flight feathers and otherwise chocolate-brown plumage.

▼

Sooty Chat 18 cm | 7"

Small, dark birds of open areas. When perched, the glossy-black males show an obvious white patch on the 'shoulders', although this is lacking in the browner females. Very similar in both appearance and behaviour to the Anteater Chat. The two species are best separated in flight: male Sooty Chats show a bold white patch at the front of the wing and the females have no white in the wing at all; Anteater Chats of both sexes show lots of white in the flight feathers (towards the end of the open wing). Pairs of Sooty Chat are usually found around large termite mounds, where they nest in the burrows of subterranean mammals.

Territorial males hold their wings down and raise their tail when singing.

Male

Female

Northern Wheatear 15 cm | 6"

A common migrant chat with an obvious white rump. This pale wheatear could be encountered between September and April almost anywhere but shows a preference for open areas. Males in spring look very smart with their grey and black plumage, while females and immatures are mostly beige. Both sexes of all ages are eye-catching in flight when the white rump flashes before you. Like other migrant wheatears, it is mostly silent in the region. This incredible bird is among the smallest of the long-distance migrants to reach East Africa and many individuals breed well inside the Arctic Circle.

Pied Wheatear 15 cm | 6"

This is a rather dark migrant wheatear with a white rump and arrives in the Serengeti from its breeding grounds in Asia and eastern Europe in September and departs by April. Males are very distinctive birds with a black face, throat and back but are otherwise very pale. Females are similar to female Northern Wheatear but appear darker brown with pale edges to the feathers in the wing. These wheatears habitually fly into trees when disturbed and are typically found in more scrubby areas than the Northern Wheatear.

The family name 'wheatear' has nothing to do with 'wheat' or 'ears' but is an old English corruption of 'white-arse' on account of the conspicuous white rump.

◀ ▢ **Capped Wheatear** 17cm | 6¾"

An attractive chat of short grass plains. With its distinctive face pattern and upright stance, the Capped Wheatear is difficult to confuse with any of the other resident bird. It is found singly or in pairs in areas of open, short grass with scattered rocks, often close to Maasai villages. It routinely bobs and pumps its tail. In flight, birds show an obvious white rump that contrasts with an all-black tail; this distinctive pattern is noticeable from afar. The sexes look similar. The two other wheatears featured here are common seasonal migrants from Europe and Asia but neither shows an all-black tail and both lack the distinctive face pattern of the Capped Wheatear.

Male

Pied Wheatear

Female

67

Longclaws get their name from the very long claw at the back of the foot.

Male

Yellow-throated Longclaw

Female

Yellow-throated Longclaw 22 cm | 8¾"

A yellow-breasted, terrestrial bird with a preference for long grass plains. It is common across the Serengeti and NCA and easily identified by its bright plumage. Females and immatures are duller than males but still show some yellow on the front. Birds are often seen along tracks and are easily flushed into the air when they glide on sharply flicked, flat wings and reveal two white squares on the end of the tail. They can be difficult to follow in grass when they have their brown, streaked back towards you. The high-pitched call "*wi-pi-pi-pi*" is frequently heard in flight.

Rosy-breasted Longclaw 20 cm | 8"

A beautiful pink-fronted bird of long grass plains. Less common and far shyer than the Yellow-throated Longclaw, the male Rosy-breasted is one of the prettiest birds in the Serengeti and NCA. Females and immatures show less pink than adult males but all birds have whiter edges to the back and flight feathers than the Yellow-throated Longclaw, giving the bird a more scalloped appearance. A white bar in the wing can often be seen in flight.

Immature male

Pipits can be a difficult group of birds to identify and, until recently, the Buffy Pipits of the Serengeti-Mara ecosystem were considered to be a race of Plain-backed Pipit – so be aware that few other field guides show Buffy Pipit occurring in this part of Tanzania.

☐ Grassland Pipit 16 cm | 6"

The common streaky-backed pipit of open grassland. This species is most often encountered on short grass plains, whereas the similar Buffy Pipit tends to prefer longer grass. The Grassland Pipit is more sedate in its locomotion (it rarely pumps its tail like a wagtail) and prefers to creep rather than run. This pipit shows heavy streaking on the back and breast and usually an obvious dark line (or moustachial stripe) from the bill to below the cheeks, a feature that is poorly marked in Buffy Pipit. In flight it shows clean white outer tail feathers

▼

☐ Buffy Pipit 17 cm | 6½"

The common plain-backed pipit of open grassland. A very erect, long-legged bird that habitually makes short dashes before braking suddenly with a pumped tail (like a wagtail). Unlike the similar Grassland Pipit, the back of this species is poorly marked and may even appear entirely plain, while the breast is lightly mottled and the belly whitish, although some birds show a warm buffy patch along the flanks. The flight is strong and reveals off-white outer tail feathers.

▼

Yellow Bishop 15 cm | 6" ▼

Short-tailed, black birds with bright-yellow flashes of the grassland edge. Males are very similar to Yellow-mantled Widowbird and both have black body plumage with a yellow 'shoulder' patch. However, male Yellow Bishops always show a bright yellow rump in all plumages and never a long, black tail. Yellow Bishops are more likely to be encountered close to water and in areas of tall, wet grass. Here you are likely to see their energetic display flight, which involves jumping from a perch and flapping rapidly before dropping down. During this show, males puff up their yellow rumps and call a rapid high-pitched *"tli-tli-tli-tli"*.

Yellow-mantled Widowbird ▼

21 cm | 8¼"

Long-tailed, black birds of the long grass plains, with bright-yellow flashes. Pairs and small groups are often flushed from long grass quite unexpectedly and will often perch on small bushes. In flight, the yellow upper-back and 'shoulder' patches of the breeding male help to separate it from Jackson's Widowbird and other wandering widowbirds such as White-winged Widowbird (which shows a yellow 'shoulder' and a white upperwing patch) and Fan-tailed Widowbird (which has a red 'shoulder' and upperwing patch) (*neither shown*). As with Jackson's Widowbird, females and non-breeding males can be very difficult to identify with certainty.

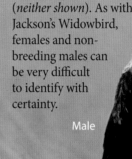

Male

Yellow-mantled Widowbird

Male

Non-breeding male

Yellow Bishop

Female Yellow Bishop

☐ Jackson's Widowbird 30 cm | 12" ▼

Dark birds of long grass plains, with long, drooping tails.

The Serengeti-Mara ecosystem is home to a very important population of these scarce birds that depend on large tracts of moist, open grassland. Breeding males are blackish with brown 'shoulder' patches and sickle-shaped tail feathers. Look out for displaying birds between January and May (during the second rains) when they fly up from the long grass before parachuting down again. Females and non-breeding males are brown and stripy and incredibly difficult to separate from other female and non-breeding male widowbirds and bishops. Flocks are often seen flying, squadron-like, several feet above the grass. This species is endemic to East Africa (*i.e.* it is only found here).

Named after Sir Frederick Jackson (1859–1929), an English administrator, explorer and ornithologist who became the first Governor of Kenya.

Widowbirds are named after their black 'lady-in-mourning' plumage.

Display flight

Male

Female

Greater Flamingo 145 cm | 57"

A very tall flamingo with a bi-coloured bill. These birds have incredibly long necks in relation to their body size and, although always taller than Lesser Flamingo, there is a huge variation in size between the taller males and the females. The best feature for separating this species from Lesser Flamingo is the colour of the bill, which is pale pink at the base and black at the tip. When the bird is on the ground, the plumage appears very pale pink, apart from the upper parts of the wings that are bright crimson-pink. Immature birds of both flamingo species are greyish-white. Birds in the air show a two-tone 'crimson-black' wing-colour combination.
Both species call a goose-like "honk".

Two of the world's six Flamingo species inhabit Africa and they are both found in East Africa, although Lesser Flamingo is frequently the most numerous in the Serengeti and NCA. The main nesting site for both flamingo species is Lake Natron, which is only about 100 km north-east of the Ngorongoro Crater, where over half a million nests can be occupied. Both species lay a single white egg on a raised mud mound and the young hatch with a straight rather than a kinked bill.

The Greater Flamingo is the state bird of Gujarat, India.

Lesser Flamingo

Greater Flamingo

The Phoenix and the Whale: In much the same way that baleen whales filter plankton, flamingos filter a protein-rich soup of mud, salt-water, algae and invertebrates using a specialized tool that is unique to the family. Within the bill are rows of bristles, called lamellae, which are used in conjunction with the rough tongue to extract the food items that pass through it, such as blue-green algae, brine shrimps and tiny molluscs. Carotenoid proteins are extracted from this diet by liver enzymes and it is these that give the flamingo its fabulous pink colouration. The scientific genus for the Greater Flamingo, *Phoenicopterus*, translates from Ancient Greek to 'crimson-wing' but you may also detect from this name the Phoenix, a mythical creature that seems to have been inspired by the flamingo.

■ Lesser Flamingo
90 cm | 36"
A short flamingo with an all-dark bill. With its proportionately thicker neck, this flamingo is not just substantially shorter than the Greater Flamingo but is also less spindly in its overall appearance. Although there is considerable variation between individuals, adults of this species are generally much pinker than Greater Flamingo but, if seen well, it is the all-dark bill that is the best identification feature. In flight, birds show a three-tone colour combination of crimson-white-black in the open wings.

☐ **Woolly-necked Stork** 86 cm | 34"

An unobtrusive dark stork with a white neck and belly. This bird is relatively scarce in the Serengeti and NCA, with wandering birds turning up on marshes and rivers throughtout the year, particularly on the Grumeti and Mara Rivers. When seen standing, look out for the purple gloss on the back of this bird. In flight, the white neck separates it from the similar Abdim's Stork (*page 37*), which is a similar size and also has a white rump.

▼

Woolly-necked Stork

Yellow-billed Stork

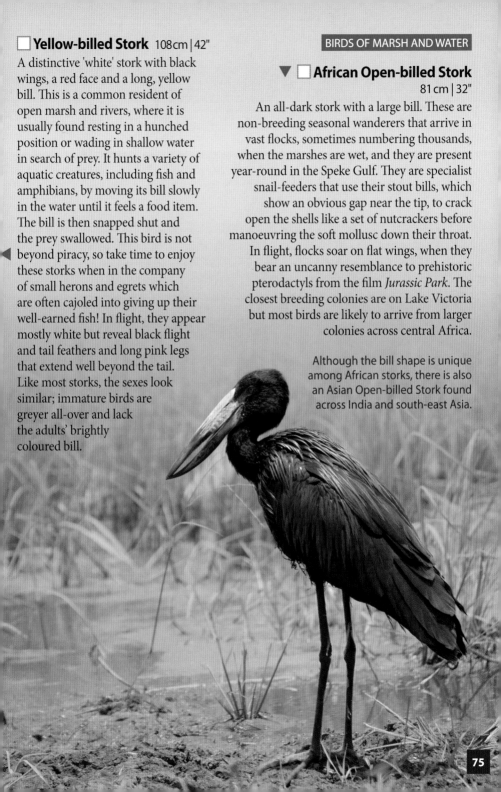

Yellow-billed Stork 108 cm | 42"

A distinctive 'white' stork with black wings, a red face and a long, yellow bill. This is a common resident of open marsh and rivers, where it is usually found resting in a hunched position or wading in shallow water in search of prey. It hunts a variety of aquatic creatures, including fish and amphibians, by moving its bill slowly in the water until it feels a food item. The bill is then snapped shut and the prey swallowed. This bird is not beyond piracy, so take time to enjoy these storks when in the company of small herons and egrets which are often cajoled into giving up their well-earned fish! In flight, they appear mostly white but reveal black flight and tail feathers and long pink legs that extend well beyond the tail. Like most storks, the sexes look similar; immature birds are greyer all-over and lack the adults' brightly coloured bill.

▼ African Open-billed Stork
81 cm | 32"

An all-dark stork with a large bill. These are non-breeding seasonal wanderers that arrive in vast flocks, sometimes numbering thousands, when the marshes are wet, and they are present year-round in the Speke Gulf. They are specialist snail-feeders that use their stout bills, which show an obvious gap near the tip, to crack open the shells like a set of nutcrackers before manoeuvring the soft mollusc down their throat. In flight, flocks soar on flat wings, when they bear an uncanny resemblance to prehistoric pterodactyls from the film *Jurassic Park*. The closest breeding colonies are on Lake Victoria but most birds are likely to arrive from larger colonies across central Africa.

Although the bill shape is unique among African storks, there is also an Asian Open-billed Stork found across India and south-east Asia.

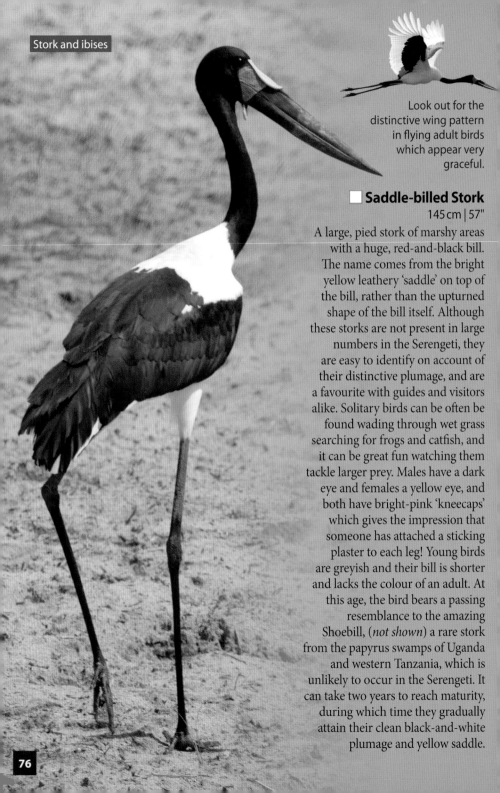

Look out for the distinctive wing pattern in flying adult birds which appear very graceful.

■ Saddle-billed Stork
145 cm | 57"

A large, pied stork of marshy areas with a huge, red-and-black bill. The name comes from the bright yellow leathery 'saddle' on top of the bill, rather than the upturned shape of the bill itself. Although these storks are not present in large numbers in the Serengeti, they are easy to identify on account of their distinctive plumage, and are a favourite with guides and visitors alike. Solitary birds can be often be found wading through wet grass searching for frogs and catfish, and it can be great fun watching them tackle larger prey. Males have a dark eye and females a yellow eye, and both have bright-pink 'kneecaps' which gives the impression that someone has attached a sticking plaster to each leg! Young birds are greyish and their bill is shorter and lacks the colour of an adult. At this age, the bird bears a passing resemblance to the amazing Shoebill, (*not shown*) a rare stork from the papyrus swamps of Uganda and western Tanzania, which is unlikely to occur in the Serengeti. It can take two years to reach maturity, during which time they gradually attain their clean black-and-white plumage and yellow saddle.

Sacred Ibis 73 cm | 29"

A wandering bird of the wetlands that can sometimes be seen in flocks of 20 or more. The general impression of an ibis is that it has a rather 'horizontal' posture, especially in comparison to the 'vertical' storks and herons that they superficially resemble. They are generally active feeders and will walk around wet and grassy areas probing their thick, strongly decurved bill in search of frogs, fish and invertebrates. The head of adult birds is jet-black and lacks feathers, but immature birds can show some white mottling on the face and neck. In flight, birds often show bare, red skin along the front of the underwings, making them appear quite prehistoric.

The bird acquired its 'Sacred' name on account of its religious status among the Pharaohs of ancient Egypt who worshipped the bird in the form of the God they named Thoth. In Saqqara, in one excavated tomb alone, 1,500,000 mummified ibises were discovered!

▶

Hadada Ibis 82 cm | 32"

A noisy brown ibis of river, marsh and, sometimes, open woodland. The bird gets its name from the very loud calls that are usually the first clue to its presence – a raucous "*haa-hahaa*," or sometimes a single drawn out "*haaaaa*". On first impression, the bird can appear a bland brown, but sit and watch and the sunlight reflecting off the wings may reveal a stunning glossy sheen of blue, green, purple and copper; this can often be seen clearly when the bird is in flight. Like the Sacred Ibis, Hadada will spend much of their time walking and probing for food. Adult birds have a whitish eye and a pale moustache extending from the red-topped bill. Look out for the similar, but scarce, Glossy Ibis (*not shown*) which is a much slimmer, darker brown version with longer legs and an all-dark bill.

These birds are very much at home in the company of people, and across southern Africa are commonly found in gardens and parks. ▼

A Hamerkop's call, usually given in flight, is a high-pitched "*chink-chink, chink*". This sounds like a hammer striking an anvil and is how the bird acquired its local name of 'fundi chuma', the blacksmith.

☐ Hamerkop 56 cm | 22" ▲

A small brown hammer-headed heron. The Hamerkop (Dutch and Afrikaans for Hammer Head) is an oddity among African herons because of its all-brown colouration, peculiar head-shape and short legs. However, like other members of the heron family, it is an accomplished fisherman and is often found at the water's edge waiting for frogs and fish to come within striking distance. It also employs other tactics such as wiggling its feet in the mud to stir up food items, and may even fly into the wind at low level and dip at the water's surface to pick off unsuspecting fish. This bird builds a huge nest in a strong tree to which it adds new extensions year after year. These constructions offer apartments for other birds, such as sparrows and weavers, and once neglected by the owners, are frequently taken over by Grey Kestrels and other species.

☐ Striated Heron 40 cm | 15¾"

A small, dark heron of pools and quiet rivers. Its body plumage is mostly grey but it has pale feather edges, subtle white stripes in the face and a black cap that is erected when the bird is excited or agitated. In the breeding season, its legs change from yellow to pink. Immature birds are similar but heavily streaked on the throat and spotted on the back and wings. In flight, the short legs and tail are obvious, and this is when you are most likely to hear its call – a short, sharp, barking growl. Although this heron is widespread across much of Tanzania, little is known of its breeding habits because it is so secretive.

☐ Squacco Heron 46 cm | 18" ▼

A small, pale heron of open marshes with white wings. Common on the shores of Lake Victoria, the Squacco Heron is a regular wanderer to the marshes of the Serengeti where it is most likely to be found along the edges of open water. Appearing short and rather bull-necked, birds in breeding plumage are beige with long cinnamon plumes down the back and a series of black and white plumes emerging from the neck. Immature and non-breeding birds are typically more streaky and have a darker-brown back. In flight, birds of all ages reveal snow-white wings and tail that contrast with the browner colouration of the back.

Squacco Heron
Non-breeding

Breeding

Non-breeding

Usually encountered in a hunched position, the Striated, or Green-backed Heron is a shy bird that prefers keeping to cover around water.

79

☐ Goliath Heron 152cm | 60"

A huge, chestnut-headed and grey-backed heron of quiet waters. With its huge, dagger-shaped bill and gigantic proportions, this really is an impressive bird by anyone's standards. In flight, look out for the rich-chestnut underwing and very broad wings. It is not likely to be confused with any other bird and all good safari guides will know it well. Take time to enjoy this bird fishing and, if it appears to be resting, you may be lucky enough to watch it sunbathing, when it stands facing the sun with its wings held half-open.

▶

The Goliath Heron is the largest heron in the world and named after the biblical giant defeated by David.

☐ Grey Heron 100cm | 38"

A large, white-and-grey heron of open water and marsh. Adult birds are easily identified by their whitish head, neck and belly, and sport long, black feathers that extend from above the eye down the back of the neck. Immature birds show more grey in the face and lack the adults' black facial plumes. In flight, birds show darker flight feathers on the upperwing, while the underwing is uniform grey with no contrast. An accomplished fisherman, the Grey Heron is not beyond taking other prey such as reptiles, young birds and small mammals. The commonly heard call is a loud "*fronk*".

▼

☐ **Black-headed Heron** 92 cm | 36"

A mostly dark, medium-sized heron of marshes and plains. Smaller and darker than the Grey Heron, this species shows a white throat that contrasts markedly with the darker head and back of the neck. In flight, the upperwing is darker than in Grey Heron and the underwing shows an obvious contrast between the white coverts (front half of wing) and blackish flight feathers (back half of wing). Often found on open marshes with other herons, the Black-headed Heron is also readily seen walking the grassy plains in search of lizards and snakes. Because this heron has a slower and less deadly approach to killing snakes, than the Secretarybird, for example, it is not uncommon to see the snake wrapping itself around the bird's bill – making for spectacular wildlife viewing!

▶

Grey Heron

Black-headed Heron

Breeding

Little Egret   Great White
Egret

Cattle Egret 56 cm | 22"

A small, short-necked, white egret that associates with grazing animals. Often found on the grassy plains where they feed among herds of Buffalo, Elephant and other large grazers, these egrets will routinely visit rivers and marshes, where they often roost. It is here where they may be confused with other egrets that are associated with water, but this is the only egret that habitually gathers in large flocks. Cattle Egrets have far shorter necks than the other species shown here, and are usually seen hunched when roosting. When breeding, birds develop bright-orange tones to the crest and chest, bright-red facial skin and orange legs. Non-breeding birds have black legs and all-white plumage.

Look out for flocks of Cattle Egrets gathering at the feet of Buffalo, where they feed on invertebrates disturbed by the mammals; they are also often seen riding on the backs of Buffalo and other large grazing animals.

Cattle Egret

Little Egret 64 cm | 25"

A medium-sized, white heron with a slim, black bill. The Little Egret is a delicate bird of open marshes, rivers and the edge of Lake Victoria, and has many similarities to the Great White Egret. However, it always shows black legs with bright-yellow feet, and a fine, black bill that contrasts with a yellow patch of skin in front of the eyes. A good view will also reveal a long, elegant crest. This species has a rarely seen 'dark morph' plumage that is slaty-grey all-over except for a white chin.

Non-breeding

Great White Egret 92cm | 36"

A large, elegant and long-necked white heron of quiet waterways. Unlike the Cattle Egret, this is predominantly a solitary bird rarely seen away from water. Although it is the largest of the white egrets, attention still needs to be paid in order to secure a positive identification. Look out for the long neck that should show a strong kink, sometimes two, and the line of the bill opening, known as the gape, which extends below and well behind the eye. As with other egrets, the plumage varies slightly according to the time of year. Birds in breeding plumage show a greenish patch of skin at the base of a black bill, long white plumes flowing from the back and breast, and yellowish legs. Non-breeding birds have an all-yellow bill, blacker legs and lack the elegant white plumes.

Little Egret

Egrets derive their name from the French word aigrette, meaning brush, on account of the long filamentous plumes they acquire in the breeding season.

☐ African Fish Eagle 73 cm | 29"

A stunning large eagle of lake, river and marsh. The quintessential sound of African waterways, the loud cry of the African Fish Eagle is never to be forgotten – adult birds throw their necks back in joy as the yelping "*weeoww-ow-ow*" call pierces the sky. The distinctive plumage of adult birds should pose no issues with identification. However, immature birds can appear a strange mix of brown and white patches, and only acquire the classic white head after several years. It is common to see these majestic birds soaring on broad wings over wet areas or perched on a conspicuous branch near water.

Although the main prey is fish, these eagles will also take lizards and birds as large as flamingos.

Adult

Immature

☐ Red-billed Teal
48 cm | 19"

This medium-sized duck is easily identified by the mostly brown plumage and dark-brown cap that contrasts with the off-white cheeks. The red bill, which shows a black line running down the centre, is a useful identification feature although it can become obscured when the bird has been dabbling in mud. In flight it shows a broad, cream patch at the rear of the wing. It feeds mostly at night but is easy to find, roosting and preening, by day.

☐ White-faced Whistling Duck 48 cm | 19"

Usually encountered in small flocks, this medium-sized, upright duck with a white face is at home along the grassy margins of open marsh and quiet rivers; it is less frequently seen along the busy stretches of the Grumeti and Mara Rivers. It has a distinctive call, a sweetly whistled "*wer-wi-wooo*", which you are likely to hear before you see the bird. They are long-necked and long-legged, and a good view will present no identification problems. However, distant birds in flight could be confused with the Fulvous Whistling Duck although that species lacks the white face and is paler chestnut-brown on the head, breast and belly. If you see a white crescent on the rump in flight then it is definitely a Fulvous. The sexes look similar in both species.

The term 'fulvous' means yellowish-brown.

■ Fulvous Whistling Duck 51 cm | 20" ▲

An attractive brown duck that is structurally very similar to its close relative the White-faced Whistling Duck. The plumage is subtle and understated although the white plumes on the flanks are rather ornate. Often seen at rest during the day, this species is most active at night, when the two-note whistle is more frequently heard. Although it can be seen in the Serengeti in small numbers throughout the year, this duck does not breed locally and most are visitors from southern Africa.

87

Spur-winged Goose 100 cm | 39"

An unmistakable large, pied goose with a white face and pink legs. This is a regular visitor to the flooded grasslands of the Serengeti and NCA but is unlikely to breed locally. The black on the back and neck appears glossy green in strong light, contrasting with the white belly. At close range, look out for the warty face and a fleshy red knob on the forehead of the male. In flight, the black upperwing has a white leading-edge and the underwing shows black flight feathers against white. Often calls in flight, a hiccup-like "*ku-wup-up*".

The Spur-winged Goose is not popular among hunters on account of its bad-tasting flesh.

Knob-billed Duck

male 76 cm | 30"; female 56 cm | 22"

A medium-sized pied waterfowl with a white neck. The strange appendage after which this species is named is only found on the bill of male birds and swells during the breeding season. Although the sexes are otherwise similar, there is a substantial size difference with females being on average about two-thirds the size of males. In flight, the wings appear all-dark from above and below, unlike the similar Spur-winged Goose that shows a great deal of white under the wing and on the leading edge.

Egyptian Goose

74 cm | 29"

A common, light-brown goose with a dark eye-patch, which is a regular feature on game drives that include rivers and marsh but is also found in grasslands. It is an attractive goose that probably looks its best in flight, when it shows a large white panel on the upperwing and iridescent green inner flight feathers. Despite their rather serene appearance, these geese can be very aggressive and fights are common where territorial incursions occur. Intruders are threatened with open wings in a show of intimidation followed by noisy honking that quickens in excitement.

Egyptian Goose   **Spur-winged Goose**

Female

Male

The frequently seen goslings are soft and downy, patched with brown and white, but turn brown and look scruffy as they age.

☐ Black-winged Stilt 38 cm | 15"

A very long-legged, elegant, black-and-white wader of open marshes. Needless to say, their extra-long, rosy-pink legs explain the name 'stilt' and enable them to feed in deeper water than other wading birds of the same size. Although a non-breeding bird in the Serengeti, it is not unusual to see them wading gracefully through shallow water on open marshes, dipping their long, thin bill from side to side or picking insects off grass stems. In flight they are readily identified by the all-white head and body contrasting sharply with the black wings – and those gangly legs extending well beyond the tail. Immatures are similar but are browner and have duller legs. The distinctive call is a dripping "*kip-kip-kip*".

Some adult birds show a dark smudge on the head.

☐ African Jacana 31 cm 12¼"

An attractive waterbird with incredibly long toes. Commonly known as the Lily-trotter on account of its habit of walking on floating vegetation, especially water-lilies, the African Jacana shows an attractive blue bill and shield on the forehead. Its breeding behaviour is particularly strange because the typical roles of the sexes are reversed. The larger females are outrageously flirtatious and frequently mate with several partners. The smaller males are the ones that build the nest, incubate the eggs and rear the young, quite independently of the female. This rare behaviour is known as polyandry. Look out for them in weak fluttering flight when they appear to be 'all-feet'.

☐ Black Crake 20 cm 8"

A shy black bird of the water's edge. These small birds rarely allow prolonged views or a close approach but, if seen well, look out for the bright yellow bill and pink legs. They prefer to remain hidden in dense vegetation but lucky observers may see them on the backs of Hippo where they feed on skin parasites. When trying to locate this bird, listen out for the unmistakable call, a muffled, ▼ dove-like "*crr-crrr-crrr-coo*".

Large plovers within the scientific genus *Vanellus*, including those here and on *pages 32–33* are also known as lapwings.

☐ **African Wattled Plover** 34 cm | 13½"

A large, brown plover with distinctive facial skin. This plover lacks the obvious patches of black and white of the pied plovers *opposite*, and appears uniform brown from a distance. Close inspection reveals a delicately streaked head and neck, and spectacular yellow wattles hanging from between the eyes and the bill, a yellow bill tipped with black and long, yellow legs. The sexes look similar but males generally have longer wattles. This plover is less restricted to open water than similar species and is often at home close to puddles and wet grass. Calling birds usually start with a prolonged series of high-pitched "*wherp*" notes but when several individuals join in excitedly it can quicken to "*wit-wit-wit-wu*".

☐ **Blacksmith Plover** 31 cm | 12¼" ▶

A common pied plover with a white forehead and black back. This bird may also be found on the edge of the plains and along the rivers throughout the reserve and surrounding area. It is the only plover to show black cheeks extending to the breast. In flight, it appears mostly grey-and-black and also shows a white rump contrasting with the black tail – the latter is a feature common to most species in the genus *Vanellus*. The name derives from its call which, like the Hamerkop, sounds like a hammer striking an anvil: "*tink-tink-tink*". It is thought to be declining in some areas due to competition from Spur-winged Plover, which is expanding its range southwards.

☐ Spur-winged Plover 28 cm | 11"

A common pied plover with white cheeks and a brown back.
This plover is easy to identify because of its bold plumage – so
you don't need to worry about seeing the bony spurs on the
wings, after which it is named, as these are usually hidden.
Even in flight, the white cheeks stand out against the dark
breast but, if seen from above, look for the white bar running
from the front to the back of the upperwing (see *page 32*).
Its call is similar to but higher pitched than that of the
Blacksmith Plover, birds often getting carried away
with excitement, especially when mating.

If you are not 100%
certain about your
identification, check
the brown *Vanellus*
plovers found on the
plains (*pages 32–33*).

▼

☐ Water Thick-knee 41 cm | 16"

A medium-sized, rather shy wading bird of the water's edge. Although quite common along rivers and in marshes in the Serengeti and NCA, these birds can be tricky to find as they tend to sit motionless rather than fly away from danger or disturbance. If seen well on the ground, look out for the crouched, horizontal posture, large yellow eyes and green legs. Once airborne, the open wings show large white patches. Birds become very active after dark and this is when they are most likely to be heard, screaming a long series of excited "*wee*" notes, starting quickly and rising to a crescendo; this sometimes involves several individuals.

Thick-knees are very spirited birds and show great valour when defending their eggs and chicks against predators, such as huge monitor lizards, by opening their wings and making darting runs to intimidate them.

Thick-knees are also known as dikkops across much of southern Africa, while the migratory Eurasian Thick-knee, a very rare visitor to the Serengeti, is also known as the Stone-curlew.

Ruff male 30 cm | 12"; female 25 cm | 10"

A common smallish brown wader of open marsh and lakeside, and sometimes short grass plains. This is among the most numerous of all shorebirds that occur in the Serengeti and NCA between September and April. When in Tanzania, most Ruff have a grey-brown back and breast, a white belly and orange legs but there is considerable variation between males and females and immatures. Males are usually 20% larger than females and often show more white in the head and more brightly coloured legs, while immatures arriving in September–October appear buffy below with rusty-brown tones on the crown and back. Most male birds (*inset*) will have reached their breeding grounds in northern Europe, some even within the Arctic Circle, by the time they acquire their stunning breeding plumage. This includes a fabulous 'ruff' of feathers around the neck which is raised to impress females – and is, of course, how the bird acquired its name.

Immature

Male in non-breeding plumage

Female (or Reeve)

Male in breeding plumage

☐ Common Greenshank 32 cm | 12½"

A medium-sized, elegant wader of the water's edge. This mostly grey-brown sandpiper is very pale on the underparts and usually shows green legs, or 'shanks' – hence its name – although very occasionally some individuals may show yellowish legs. The long bill shows a slight but obvious upward curve and becomes darker towards the tip. Greenshanks are energetic feeders and swing their bill from side to side through the water; they will also often run through the shallows chasing small fish and invertebrates. In flight they appear dark above and pale below with an obvious white triangle running up the back. The resonant "*chew-chew-chew*" call is very distinctive and often alerts you to the bird well before you have seen it.

This is the largest of the migratory sandpipers that breed in northern Europe and visit the Serengeti and NCA during the northern winter. It is usually found here from September until April but some birds stay throughout the year.

☐ Marsh Sandpiper 25 cm | 10"

An elegant and leggy migrant sandpiper with a fine, black bill. A close relative of the Common Greenshank, this species can usually be separated by its thinner, needle-like, straight black bill and overall slimmer appearance. Freshly arrived immature birds may sometimes show yellowish legs and a yellowish base to the bill, but the bill is always slimmer than that of the Greenshank. Adults of both species show greenish legs but in Marsh Sandpiper they appear relatively longer and in flight extend much further beyond the tail. Also in flight, both species show an obvious white wedge extending from the tail up the back.

☐ Three-banded Plover 18 cm | 7"

A small plover with two – not three – dark bands across the breast. If you are wondering why it is called Three-banded Plover, just remember that the white band between the two black ones also counts! This attractive little wader, with its bright red eye-rings and pink legs, is often very confiding and allows a close approach, especially in muddy roadside pools. It is also common along sandy river banks where your attention may be drawn to its very high-pitched "*phew-eet*" contact call. When very excited it calls a long, muffled "*wi-wi-sher-wir-wirrit*" that sounds rather like a swift.

General note: these small sandpipers are all seasonal migrants from Europe and Siberia and can be difficult to separate. When observing them, pay particular attention to their calls and the following three features: rump and tail pattern; leg colour; and the degree of contrast between the upperparts and underparts.

◀ ☐ Wood Sandpiper 20 cm | 8"

A refined sandpiper of flooded grass, rivers and marshes. Wood Sandpipers are far more numerous than Green Sandpipers and are often, but not always, encountered in small flocks. They lack the strong contrast in plumage of the Green Sandpiper, primarily because the back and wings have numerous pale markings and the sides of the belly carry some soft barring. This combines to give the bird a more streaked appearance and less 'black-and-white'. The bright yellowish-green legs are a very useful identification feature. In flight, this wader shows a pale-grey underwing and a gentle intergrade between the mottled back and the white rump, while the tail shows several narrow bars. The monotone call "*chif-if-if*" is a common feature of wet areas throughout much of the year but birds become scarce between May and August.

◀ ☐ Green Sandpiper 23 cm | 9"

A stocky sandpiper of quiet waters. The Green Sandpiper is most similar to Wood Sandpiper but shows far greater contrast between the dark back and wings, which have little in the way of pale flecking, and the white belly. The face is usually quite dark, making the white eye-ring quite prominent if seen well; it lacks a pale eyebrow extending beyond the eye, which is a feature of Wood Sandpiper. Both the bill and the legs are dark and greenish. In flight, birds appear blackish, especially on the underwing, and show a contrasting clean white rump and three to four strong black bars running across the end of the tail. Rising birds call a piercing "*tlu-EET-wit-wit*" that is far more abrupt than the Wood Sandpiper.

◀ ☐ Common Sandpiper 18 cm | 7½"

A small, short-legged, hunched sandpiper with a brown tail and rump. It is a migrant and occurs commonly between August and May, being found mainly along boulder-strewn streams, although birds will also visit wider rivers and marshes. It stands with a horizontal posture and walks with a bobbing action, regularly 'pumping' its rear-end. Unlike the other two sandpipers shown here, the Common Sandpiper's tail projects well beyond the wing-tips. The belly is crisp white with no barring on the flanks, and the white extends up towards the shoulder. The flight action is low and pulsating with the wings arched slightly downwards. It lacks a white rump and is uniformly brown across the back and down the tail, which is often spread and appears pointed in the centre. The open wing has a long, narrow white bar down the middle. The call is a very high-pitched long series of "*swee-swee-swee*" notes.

This is the largest of the world's 93 species of kingfisher.

▼ ☐ Giant Kingfisher 43 cm | 17"

A huge, chequered kingfisher of larger waterways. Generally scarce and shy, the Giant Kingfisher is about the size of a crow and has a thick, shaggy crest at the back of the head. Males show a chestnut breast-band, whereas females have a chestnut-coloured belly. It is quite at home along the Grumeti, Mara and smaller rivers, where it hunts fish, crabs and amphibians by diving from a perch. It is easily disturbed and calls a loud "*kark*" note, often in flight.

☐ Malachite Kingfisher 12 cm | 4½"

A brilliant blue-and-red jewel of still and slow-moving water. Despite its tiny size, the Malachite Kingfisher causes gasps of amazement because of its stunning plumage. Sometimes found balancing from a grass stem hanging over a small pool, it sits and watches for any small fish or tasty morsel to surface, snatching it with a rapid dive. It then proceeds to slam the unfortunate fish on its perch to kill it and make swallowing it, head first, easier. Otherwise, a flash of brilliant colour whizzing along the water at top speed is the typical view. The nest is made at the end of a long tunnel in a sandbank. The simple call is a soft high-pitched "*peep*".

Pied Kingfisher 25 cm | 10"

A common black-and-white kingfisher of open water. Regularly seen hovering over rivers and marshes, the Pied Kingfisher is quite unmistakable and not at all shy. Pairs and family parties are often seen together and their metallic "*chit*" contact calls are frequently heard in unison. Males are easily told from females by their two solid black bands across the chest; females show just a single, broken band. It is among the most cosmopolitan of all kingfishers, being found in south-eastern Europe and across the Middle East and southern Asia to China, as well as throughout Africa.

Female

Male

☐ Yellow Wagtail 19 cm | 7½"

A highly variable migrant wagtail. With a breeding range that covers almost all of Europe and Asia, the Yellow Wagtail is represented by many regional races, the males of which all show a distinct head pattern. Variations include white, yellow, blue, grey and black caps, but all adult males show an olive-green back and some yellow on the underside. These birds are attracted to marshes and lake shores, and to feeding herds of cattle and Buffalo, which they follow through grassland and feed on the insects that are disturbed. They gather in flocks and maintain contact with a loud, high-pitched "*sreeep*" call.

▼

☐ Common Waxbill 10 cm | 4"

A masked 'finch' of both wet and dry grassland, often close to water. Usually encountered in flocks dangling from grassy seed-heads, these dainty little birds show a bright-red waxy-looking bill, red bandit's mask and white on the chin. Otherwise they are mostly brown, though a close-up view will reveal fine barring throughout and a black belly. They are widespread in the Serengeti and NCA but move seasonally in search of the best seeding grasses – so if you see one you are likely to see many.

'Black-headed'

'Sykes's'

'Blue-headed'

'Yellow-headed'

Waxbills are very popular cage birds and many have escaped from captivity in various parts of the world. They now live wild in Brazil, Spain and Portugal and on many small islands in the Atlantic, Pacific and Indian Oceans.

Male

Immature

☐ **African Pied Wagtail** 20 cm | 8" ▲

A small, black-and-white bird with a long tail, commonly found along the edge of rivers. These dainty, strikingly plumaged birds habitually pump their tails when perched and when walking. The frequently heard call is a strong, whistled "*chereep-chup-chup-chup*", sometimes ending "*watcha watcha*".

103

Brown Snake Eagle 71 cm | 28"

A medium-sized, brown eagle with an owl-like face. The dark chocolate-brown plumage appears uniform when the bird is perched, scanning for snakes and other reptiles. It has a rounded head and forward-facing bright-yellow eyes. In flight it looks plain from above but shows very pale, almost silvery, flight feathers from below. Immature birds tend to be paler on the face but are otherwise similar to adults.

Unlike many other eagles, snake eagles have mostly bare legs that are useful when tackling dangerous snakes.

Even in a light wind, look for the floppy crest that looks like a crazy punk hairdo!

Long-crested Eagle 58 cm | 23"

The only dark-brown raptor with a long crest. Although this small, compact eagle has a preference for open woodland, it can also be encountered on the plains, when its distinctive silhouette may be seen as it perches on top of a tree. It watches patiently before dropping down to prey upon reptiles and small mammals. In addition to the long, floppy crest, its bare parts are bright-yellow and it sports short, white 'trousers'. It has a peculiar flapping flight on straight wings, which show a large white patch on the top and lots of white on the underside. The tail is dark with grey bars.

Steppe Buzzard

Brown Snake Eagle

Long-crested Eagle

☐ **Steppe Buzzard** 50 cm | 20"

A medium-sized brown raptor with a reddish tail. This common migrant from Asia arrives into the Serengeti and Crater Highlands in October and remains until March. It spends much of its time perched in open woodland, waiting for prey to pass by, although it is also an effective scavenger. Great variations in the plumage occur but the majority are brown-backed, lightly barred below and have a predominately reddish and unbarred tail. This species is also widely known as Common Buzzard but the migratory subspecies that occurs in East Africa is distinctive and may well be a species in its own right.

Buff-crested Bustard 60 cm | 24"

A small bustard with a black belly that is found in thorny scrub and arid stony desert. This bird is much smaller than the bustards on *pages 28–29* and is less at home in long grass, preferring areas with a sandy or stony substrate. Males show a buff-coloured head, including the crest that is generally relaxed but raised in display to females, and a black stripe running from the chin to the black underparts. Like all small bustards, the females are very well camouflaged. Both sexes are reluctant fliers, preferring to creep away from threats, but show a broad white patch in the wing once airborne.

▼

Spotted Thick-knee 44 cm | 17½"

A cryptically patterned medium-sized wader of dry scrub and bush. It is very obviously spotted and is often found in the shade of bushes. Like the Water Thick-knee (*page 94*), it is a reluctant flier by day and prefers to run from danger. It is primarily nocturnal and calls vociferously at night, when it can often be found on tracks and roads.

The Spotted Thick-knee lacks
the black bar across the wing
that is obvious on the Water
Thick-knee (*page 94*).

☐ Heuglin's Courser 27 cm | 10½" ▲

A remarkably camouflaged nocturnal wader of dry areas. Although it probably occurs
throughout the Serengeti and NCA, this bird is notoriously difficult to find and is only
recorded with any regularity at Ndutu and Speke Bay Lodge, where the local bird guides
know where to find it. Its plumage is not only an effective camouflage but also incredibly
beautiful and any encounter with this bird should be savoured. When termites begin to
emerge from their hills in vast numbers, these waders will break their nocturnal habits
to feast during the daytime.

Red-necked Spurfowl
38 cm | 15"

A grey-brown francolin with red bare parts. Common in lightly wooded country in the west of the Serengeti, this distinctive gamebird always shows a red bill and legs but only males exhibit the red skin on the neck. They are vocal birds, screaming out their territorial calls "*kwark-kwaark*" at any time of day. They do not have a defined breeding season and males can be seen chasing females at breakneck speed with open wings and great gusto – hilarious to watch! Not surprisingly, females lay several clutches of eggs each year.

▶

Grey-breasted Spurfowl
40 cm | 16"

A grey-brown francolin with an orange-red throat and grey legs. This species is endemic to north-west Tanzania, with its stronghold in the central Seronera area of the Serengeti, although it also reaches westwards to the Speke Gulf. Its range overlaps slightly with the similar Yellow-necked Spurfowl (where the two may sometimes interbreed) and throat colour is the best feature for separating the two. It is also similar to the Red-necked Spurfowl but can be identified by the white moustache between the facial skin and the throat and also by the grey rather than red legs. It also shows some chestnut colouration on its back, and the flanks are mottled white, black and chestnut.

General note: The names spurfowl and francolin are often used interchangeably for the same species, the actual difference being minimal. In East Africa, the name spurfowl is given to those species that show bare throat skin, and francolin to those that do not. The South Africans take a different stance, with Scaly and Hildebrandt's Francolins being called Spurfowl. It's a funny old 'game'!

Yellow-necked Spurfowl
40 cm | 16"

A scruffy brown fowl with a patch of bare yellow skin on the neck. Favouring dry grass and light scrub in the south and east of the Serengeti, this gamebird is not uncommon but can be difficult to find even though it lives in open areas. This is partly because it feeds in a crouched position, with the brightly coloured head well-hidden, and the back is well-camouflaged. It has large clutches of eggs and pairs may be seen with as many as 12 chicks at a time. However, they are heavily predated and entire broods can be lost.

☐ Helmeted Guineafowl 61 cm | 24" ▶

A large, gregarious gamebird with finely spotted plumage. Despite its bare blue-and-red skinned face and bony helmet, this is an attractive bird that feeds in the open but needs trees nearby in which to roost and take refuge from its many predators. It is a favourite with small cats, such as Serval, and stealthy birds of prey including the Martial Eagle. The chicks exhibit rapid wing growth and are able to fly from danger when they are just one week old.

☐ Coqui Francolin 28 cm | 11"

A small, rusty-coloured francolin of open scrub and grassland. This beautifully marked gamebird is often encountered on the edge of plains where the bush thickens into open woodland. Males are rusty-brown on the head and heavily barred underneath; females show dark markings on the face and a rusty breast. There is uncertainty about how this francolin got its name, but it probably stems from its call, a repeated "*ko-kee*" that rises to a crescendo. This is most often heard in the late afternoon.

▼

Female

Male

Across East Africa, the Kiswahili name for Helmeted Guineafowl is Kanga, a name that is also given to the colourful spotted cloth often worn by women as a sarong.

▼ ■ Crested Francolin
30 cm | 12"

A stripy, bantam-like gamebird. This drab francolin has a preference for dry, open scrub and often gathers in large family groups. The sexes look similar, although females show more barring on the upperparts than males. The short crest, after which the bird is named, can be difficult to see unless birds are excited, but look out for the cocked tail that is usually raised, especially when running.

'Collared' doves

☐ Ring-necked Dove 25cm | 10"

A common beige-coloured dove of lightly wooded areas. The black collar at the back of the neck, after which this bird is named, is distinctive, but this feature is also shared with the larger Red-eyed and African Mourning Dove. In flight, the upperwing shows a pale-grey stripe that contrasts with the darker flight feathers, and the light-brown tail has white triangles at each corner – a useful identification aid when the bird flies away. The well-loved call is one of the easiest of all to remember, a softly purred "*pur-PUR-pur*", commonly translated to "*work harder*" (mornings) or "*more lager*" (evenings). It is known as the Cape Turtle Dove across southern Africa.

☐ Red-eyed Dove 32cm | 12½"

A large, dark-brown dove with a black collar and a bright rosy flush. More restricted to wooded areas than the Ring-necked Dove, this species is a rich dark-brown on the back, has grey on the belly and, in flight, shows a smoky-grey tail with a thick blackish band across the middle. Although the red eye and eye-ring can be difficult to see, the pink flush to the neck and breast is obvious and contrasts with the white forehead. Its call is a bouncy series of purred notes that usefully translates to "*I am a Red-eyed Dove*", often repeated over and over.

☐ African Mourning Dove 30cm | 12"

The common beige-coloured dove at Lake Victoria. This dove is usually found close to water especially in the west of the Serengeti. It is very similar to the widespread Ring-necked Dove but shows blue tones on the head, a bright-red eye-ring and a pale iris. In addition to a number of coo-ing notes, this bird has a fantastic call that is unforgettable once heard, a downward purring "*AAA-ooooowww*".

Collared Doves of the Serengeti and NCA

These three species may appear very similar at first but once you 'get your eye in' they can easily be separated. Among the best features to check on any birds seen are the general colour tone (Red-eyed appears darker than the others with a rosy flush to the plumage), eye colour (both Red-eyed and Ring-necked Doves appear dark but Mourning Dove is obviously pale with conspicuous red rings around the eyes), and overall size (Red-eyed is largest and Ring-necked is smallest). In flight, only Red-eyed Dove lacks an obvious white tip to the tail. Finally, habitat preference can also be very useful. If you spend just a few minutes getting familiar with the birds you see well, you will be identifying these species like an expert in no time!

☐ **Speckled Pigeon** 34 cm 13½"

A large, heavily spotted pigeon, common around villages surrounding the Serengeti and NCA, as well as in wooded gardens around camps and lodges. The brown wings are peppered with white spots and in flight the rump shows as pale-grey and the tail is bordered with black. The grey head contrasts with a patch of bare red skin around the eyes, and the chest is delicately streaked with maroon. Just like urban pigeons, this bird has a habit of clapping its wings on take-off.

▶

◀ ☐ African Green Pigeon
27 cm | 10½"

A spectacular bright-green pigeon. Usually found feeding in the top of fruiting trees, especially fig, these gorgeous lime-green birds have a peculiar call that is quite unlike that of other pigeons and doves. It starts with a soft "*hoo-hoo-wee-oo*" followed by excited whinnying and a few yelped "*whip-hoo-woo-whip*" notes before ending softly with "*ku-KU-ku-ku*". If you are lucky enough to see it well, look out for the red bill with a white tip and the lilac shoulder-patch. As they depend on emerging fruits, birds will commute great distances from their roosting sites to visit favoured fruiting trees.

The infamously extinct Dodo of Mauritius in the Indian Ocean was a giant flightless pigeon, closely related to the green pigeons. It became island-bound as the commuting distance between island and mainland became too great over millions of years.

☐ Emerald-spotted Wood Dove
20 cm | 8"

A small, colourful dove of dry, wooded areas, usually seen running around on the woodland floor with an action similar to a clockwork toy. If disturbed it shoots into the air with a rapid burst of wing-beats, showing chestnut flight feathers and a grey rump and tail with narrow black bars. The frequently heard call is a series of muffled "*coo*" notes that start with a rise (exactly like the first four notes of *Rule Britannia* for those who know it) before simultaneously falling in tone and speeding up, finishing on a rapid, pulsating flourish. This will make sense when you hear it! The glossy emerald wing-spots may appear black or shiny-blue in some lights, but be careful not to confuse this common bird with the scarce Blue-spotted Wood Dove (*not shown*) that is only found in wetter forests of the western Serengeti and has a dark-red bill with a yellow tip.

▼

▼ ☐ Namaqua Dove 25 cm | 10"

A small, slim dove of dry country with a long, pointed tail. Males have a distinctive black face, throat and breast and show a yellow-tipped red bill and glossy, bluish-purple wing spots. Young birds appear very scaly. This dove has a very fast and direct flight, when it shows chestnut-brown in the flight feathers.

Female

Male

◀ ☐ Laughing Dove 23 cm | 9"

A small, rufous-and-grey-winged dove. Common in drier areas, and often on open ground, this species still requires trees in which to nest and is rarely found far from cover. It lacks the black neck collar of a number of the other doves but has a black-and-rusty mottled patch high on the chest. In flight, it appears slender and shows large white corners to the long, dark-centred tail that are more obvious than those of Ring-necked Dove (*page 113*). It has a wide distribution, being found across most of Africa and from south-eastern Europe, where it is also known as the Palm Dove, eastwards across much of Asia. Its call is a gentle giggling "*hoo-woo-woo-woo-woo*", hence the bird's name.

☐ **Speckled Mousebird** 33 cm | 13" ▼

A small-bodied brown bird with a long, stiff tail. This comical little bird is often seen clambering through bushes and thick vegetation, where it feeds on seeds and fruit. As its name suggests, it does appear quite mouse-like, apart from in flight when its long tail is a useful identification feature. Good views will also reveal pale cheeks and pink feet. The call is a simple chatter, "*chir-chir-chir-chir-chir*" that drops in tone. Compare with the more elegant Blue-naped Mousebird (*page 168*).

Formerly known as coly-birds (the scientific genus remains *Colius*), these cute balls of feather were once given as gifts between the Lords, Ladies and gentry of the day. It is thought that the 'Four Calling Birds' alluded to in the *12 Days of Christmas* carol is a corruption from the original 'Four Coly-birds', but this changed over time because nobody knew what a coly-bird was.

Lovebirds acquired their romantic name from their habits of mutual preening and monogamous pairing, and it is not unusual to see them interlocking bills as though they are kissing. *Ahhhhh!*

Named in honour of Dr Gustav Adolf Fischer (1848–86), who also discovered the Fischer's Sparrow Lark (*page 65*)

Fischer's Lovebird 15 cm | 6" ▲

A charming and colourful small parrot of well-wooded savannah. Despite their beautiful colours, they can be tricky to find but their distinctive chittering calls are a give-away when flying in flocks overhead. Lovebirds are very sociable birds and gather in sizeable flocks to feed, preen and roost. They spend much time on the ground feeding on seeds but fly quickly at the first sign of danger, when you may see their bright-blue rumps. Natural and excavated holes in mature trees are their favoured places in which to nest.

Meyer's Parrot 23 cm | 9"

A medium-sized, brown parrot with a green belly and splashes of yellow, often seen in pairs and small family groups. Meyer's Parrot is also known as Brown Parrot, which seems a shame as it carries so many other bright colours. The noisy screeches, given in flight and when perched, mean that you are unlikely to miss it if it is around. Young birds lack the yellow on the crown but are otherwise similar to adults. It is found where fruiting trees are located, especially *Warburgia* that is abundant in riverine woodland.

Named after Dr Bernhard Meyer (1767–1836), who was a physician by profession but a keen ornithologist in his spare time. Oddly, it is believed that he never actually travelled to Africa where this species is found.

African Grey Hornbill 51 cm | 20"

A medium-sized hornbill with a white eyebrow and scaly brown plumage. This bird feeds in a variety of trees where it eats mostly fruits and invertebrates. It travels between trees and bushes with an undulating flight, when it looks like a flying walking stick on account of its slim lines and decurved bill. Birds stay in contact with long, piped calls "*kwi-kwi-kwi-KWEEo-KWEE-o*". Their breeding behaviour is remarkable: once a suitable nest hole in a tree is found, the female seals herself in to deter predators and nest-site rivals, using her droppings and other debris. She leaves a small slit through which the male feeds her during the period of incubation. When the young grow too large for comfort she leaves the nest and the chicks re-seal the entrance. Both adults then feed the chicks until they are ready to fledge.

Female

Male

Many safari guides call this the water-bottle bird because of its distinctive call, a rapid series of bubbling *"woo-woo-woo-woo"* notes that fall before rising with a stammer at the end.

▼ ☐ White-browed Coucal 41 cm | 16"

A bulky brown bird of wet and wooded areas. Closely related to the cuckoos, coucals raise their own young and make grassy, domed nests in tall grass or thick vegetation. They are weak fliers and rarely wander far from their territory. Coucals appear rather ungainly on the ground but spend much of their time walking stealthily through vegetation in search of a meal – this can include eggs and baby birds, reptiles and amphibians. In addition to being good parents, they are also good at relationships and will pair for life. If one bird dies, the other will spend days mourning for its loved one. Compare with the Blue-headed Coucal (*page 200*) that is restricted to the wetlands of Lake Victoria.

◀ ☐ Bare-faced Go-away-bird
48 cm | 19"

A large, pale-grey bird with a tall crest and long, broad tail. Often seen in pairs or groups, this go-away-bird does not scream *"Go Away"* like its southern African relative the Grey Go-away-bird. Instead it calls *"cor-cor"* very loudly and runs along the branches of trees in great excitement, often hopping from one to the next. The face is mostly black and the tall, grey crest gives the bird a comical expression which should be compared with that of the White-bellied Go-away-bird on *page 167*. It is a close relative of the turacos (*page 182*) but lacks the bright colours of those birds. The Bare-faced Go-away-bird does, however, show a greenish patch on the breast, like a wet grass stain.

Immature birds, often seen being fed by their smaller foster parents, such as this White-browed Robin Chat, are dark-brown above with a white, strongly barred belly.

Juvenile

☐ Red-chested Cuckoo ▶
30 cm | 12"

A hawk-like bird with barred underparts. Often referred to as the Rain-bird, these elusive cuckoos are a common feature of the wooded highlands of East Africa on account of their loud, three-note call "*wip-wip-weeu*", which translates as "*it will rain*". Professional meteorologists have nothing to fear, however, as these birds call during the well-known rainy seasons – and quite frequently after the rain has already started! Adults are dark-grey across the upperparts, show a pale-grey head, and have a rich-chestnut band across the chest. Like most African cuckoos, they are brood-parasites, laying their eggs in the active nests of other species, especially the White-browed Robin Chat (*above* and *page 156*).

Adult

121

Three green gems

Male

Female

Male

▲ ☐ **Klaas's Cuckoo** 18 cm | 7"

An emerald-green cuckoo of woodland and gardens. About the size of a Common Bulbul (*page 143*), this small cuckoo is a brood-parasite of the sunbird family, especially the tiny Collared Sunbird (*page 153*). Males are iridescent green on the head and mostly white on the front, whilst females are browner and heavily barred. Both sexes show a fleck of white behind the eye. In flight they reveal white outer tail feathers so could be confused with a honeyguide (*page 130*), which show the same feature. The call is unmistakable, a whistled two-note "*phwee-phuu*", the second note lower than the first, which is often repeated three times.

Named after the Khoi Khoi servant of French explorer and collector Francois Le Vaillant (1753–1824) who presumably found the bird for him. Le Vaillant also named the Bateleur (*page 47*).

Diederik Cuckoo 19 cm | 7½"

A heavily barred cuckoo with a distinctive call. This bird can be found in a variety of habitats, from open woodland to dry acacia scrub. During the wet season, from October to June, you are likely to find it close to the communal hanging nests of the Village Weaver (*page 160*), where the female cuckoo lays her eggs while the weavers are not at home. Superficially similar to the Klaas's Cuckoo, the Diederik Cuckoo is a slightly larger bird with many white spots on the wing and barring on the underparts, including the underwing in flight. The bird's name derives from its loud call, a resonant "*dee-dee-DEE-der-ick*".

A male is shown; female and immature birds are much browner on the back with heavily barred underparts.

▼ Little Bee-eater 15 cm | 6"

A colourful darting bird of open scrub. As the name suggests, these birds and most of the other species in this family specialize in a diet of bees, wasps and other insects that they catch in flight at breakneck speed. They are often found perched low down on the edge of bushes, where they wait for their prey to fly by, and call with a series of dry "*chip*" notes. They nest in a burrow in a sandy bank usually, but not always, close to water. The similar Cinnamon-chested Bee-eater (*page 184*) is a larger species preferring highland forests and shows warmer brown tones across the underparts. Also check out the migratory Eurasian Bee-eater on *page 195*.

Striped Kingfisher 17 cm | 6¾"

An unobtrusive and rather dowdy kingfisher. This bird is often found far from water, where it is a specialist hunter of grasshoppers and other sizeable invertebrates. The bill is dark above and red below – the reverse of Woodland Kingfisher – and it shows a dark mask through the eye. Like the Grey-headed Kingfisher, its blue colouration is restricted to the wings and tail. Although shy and sometimes difficult to find, the Striped Kingfisher becomes extravert during its display, when it lands on an exposed perch, opens it wings, and calls a long, pulsating "*wi-frreeeeewww*".

Woodland Kingfisher
22 cm | 8¾"

A brilliant sky-blue kingfisher with a red-and-black bill. With its bright colours, dazzling display and unforgettable call, this bird is a favourite among guides and safari-goers alike. Usually found in lightly wooded areas, the Woodland Kingfisher is the bluest of the bush kingfishers and shows a bright red upper half to the bill and black lower half. Like the Striped Kingfisher, it displays with open blue wings, and calls a penetrating "*CHEW-chhrreerrrr*". It will happily feed on small lizards and amphibians, as well as invertebrates.

General note: These kingfishers are not restricted to water and feed primarily on invertebrates rather than fish. The colour of the bill, face and back are all useful identification features and the calls are distinctive. Their scientific genus *Halcyon* stems from the mythical Alcyon bird, which produced 14 days of calm weather during the northern winter. Hence, today, Halcyon days are calm and cloud-free.

■ Grey-headed Kingfisher ▶
21 cm | 8¾"

A dark-backed kingfisher with a pale head. Often found in bush and lightly wooded areas, sometimes close to water, this kingfisher shows a grey head and breast and a chestnut belly, whilst the wing-tips and tail are bright blue – most obvious when seen in flight. Its bill is all-red, although young birds may show a dark tip. It is less vocal than the other kingfishers shown here but you may still hear the softly chipped "*tit-tit-tit-tit*" notes that comprise its call.

125

Hoopoes

Wood-hoopoes appear quite clumsy as they fly from tree to tree, preferring large and mature acacias, and stay in contact with chuckling calls.

Usually found alone or in pairs, the Common Scimitarbill is not as sociable as the similar Green Wood-hoopoe but frequents a similar habitat of open woodland.

Green Wood-hoopoe 37 cm | 14½"

A gregarious dark bird with a long tail.
Usually found in family groups, the Green Wood-hoopoe appears black on first impression, but good light will reveal an iridescent gloss to the plumage, mostly violet on the wings and tail but green on the head and back. The strong, pointed red bill shows a slight curve and is used to probe tree bark on boughs and trunks for invertebrates. The feet are red. Its long tail is dark with white spots along the outer edge. In flight, the wings show a broad white bar across the flight feathers and a single white spot at the front.

Common Scimitarbill 30 cm | 12"

A black bird with a long tail and long, decurved bill. The very fine bill is strongly curved along its entire length and is black – not red as in the wood-hoopoe. Its feet are also black (not red) and its plumage lacks any green gloss, although in excellent light you may see a purple gloss on the back. In flight, it is similar to the Green Wood-hoopoe but shows a narrow white bar in the wing and lacks the white spot at the front. It makes a soft, high-pitched "*sisisi*" contact call and a stronger run of downslurred "*werp-werp-werp*" notes when excited.

▼ Hoopoe 28 cm | 11"

A bright-orange bird with black-and-white stripes in the wing. Unmistakable, with an erectile crest, the Hoopoe can vary in colour from orange to light-brown according to the time of year. It feeds on the ground with a stitching motion, probing the ground with its decurved bill for grubs and worms. On take-off, it shows an elaborate pied decoration of stripes through the rounded wings and tail. It prefers to nest in tree holes but will also nest in stone walls or sandy banks. The call is a low, two-note or three-note series "*poop-poop-poop*" with which guides should be familiar.

☐ **Usambiro Barbet** 19 cm | 7½"

A comical yellowish bird with black and white spots. It is common where bush and scrub meet grassy plain, and is often seen sunning itself in the morning light. Barbets are close relatives of woodpeckers but this species tends to be more terrestrial in its habits. The longish tail is heavily barred, while the body is mostly yellowish with black spotting, giving the bird a rather scruffy appearance. They are often seen in pairs when they make cyclical, ratchety calls with their tails cocked proudly in the air. This bird is found only in the Serengeti-Mara ecosystem and was formerly considered to be a race of the widespread D'Arnaud's Barbet. It is, however, now considered to be a distinct species in its own right.

☐ Spot-flanked Barbet
14 cm | 5½"

A black-throated barbet of open bush and light woodland. This small barbet is usually heard before it is seen and calls a repeated series of "*kweerk*" notes that get faster with each note and sounds quite excitable. It is very fond of fruits and with prolonged observation you may see these birds regurgitate small waxy parcels of seeds onto branches or drop them on the ground. Ecologists believe that this bird, along with other fruit-eating barbets, returns a great service to its food plants by dispersing seeds.

▼

☐ Red-fronted Tinkerbird
10 cm | 4"

A small and noisy barbet of dry bush and well-wooded areas. Although mostly black and white on the head, this finch-sized barbet shows much yellow on the wings and rump. As with the much larger Red-fronted Barbet (*page 166*), the red at the front of the crown is not always easy to see, so it is better to look out for the heavily striped head and clean white throat instead. Its monotonous "*ponk-ponk-ponk*" call may be repeated 20 or more times and is an easy call to remember. The similar Yellow-fronted Tinkerbird (*not shown*) is not likely to be recorded in the Serengeti or the NCA.

▼

◼ Greater Honeyguide
19 cm | 7½"

A vocal bird of open woodland. You are likely to hear these birds making their repeated, telephone-like, territorial call "*wheet-too*" well before you see them. The first view is usually a good look at their distinctive behinds as they fly off. The flash of white in the outer tail feathers is common to both honeyguides shown here – but be wary that Klaas's Cuckoo (*page 122*) shares the same feature. The basic plumage of this species is grey below and dull brown above, but the sexes and immature birds can be told apart: males show a black throat and white cheeks; females do not; while immature birds have a bright lemon-yellow wash to the throat and breast and a blue eye-ring.

▶

Like cuckoos, honeyguides are brood-parasites, laying their eggs in other birds' nests for the host family to raise. However, honeyguides target different species, specializing in tree-hole nesters such as barbets and woodpeckers.

Male

Both sexes call a soft rattle which lures people and Honey Badgers to bee colonies, where both parties get to enjoy the spoils.

Immature

☐ Lesser Honeyguide 14 cm | 5½"

A shy sparrow-like bird with a dark, stubby bill and grey and olive-green plumage. This is a common resident of wooded areas but can be tricky to find since it often sits still for long periods. Unlike the Greater Honeyguide, it does not attract people or Honey Badgers to bee colonies – but still has a sweet tooth, enjoying beeswax and insects in equal measure – and is happy to feast on the spoils after a bees' nest has been raided by others. The call is a repeated number of "*chip*" notes.

☐ Bearded Woodpecker 23 cm | 9" ▼

A large woodpecker with a black-and-white striped face. Although widespread in areas with plenty of mature trees, this species is nowhere common. Unlike the other woodpeckers in the region, it shows dark underparts consisting of fine olive-green bars. The striped facial pattern is very obvious in both sexes. Males are identified by the bright red patch at the rear of the crown but otherwise the sexes are similar.

Male

Female

Female

**Nubian
Woodpecker**

Male

■ Green-backed Woodpecker
17 cm | 6¾"

A medium-sized, spotted woodpecker of woods and gardens. Although superficially similar to the Nubian Woodpecker, both sexes show a speckled throat (the throat is unmarked in Nubian). Like Nubian, adult males have an all-red crown but lack the red 'moustache'. They are noisy birds, often heard calling "*ker-EEK*" over and over. This species is also known as the Little Spotted Woodpecker.

Like parrots and cuckoos, woodpeckers are zygodactyl, meaning that they have two toes directed forwards and two pointing backwards. Most other birds have one backward and three forward-pointing toes.

▲ ■ Nubian Woodpecker 20 cm | 8"

A large, spotted woodpecker of open bush and acacia scrub. A common visitor to old fallen trees on the savannah, this woodpecker shows bold, dark spots on the underparts, pale spots on the upperparts with some fine, pale barring on the wings, and yellow shafts to the tail feathers. Males can be distinguished by their red cap and red 'moustache' (known as the malar stripe), whereas females show a black forehead peppered with white and no 'moustache'. Their flight is heavily undulating. Listen out for the loud call "*keek-keek-kee-kee*", which gets progressively slower and sounds like a bicycle hurtling downhill while applying bad brakes.

Cardinal Woodpecker
14 cm | 5½"

A small, streaked woodpecker of woods and gardens. This woodpecker is very approachable and is frequently found in camps and lodges. A great place to start looking for it is where a collection of animal skulls is exhibited, for they routinely feed on the insect larvae that bury inside the horn of, for example, Wildebeest, Eland and Buffalo. Unlike the other woodpeckers shown here, the underparts are streaked rather than spotted, and the back and wings show pale barring. The name Cardinal derives from the male's red cap, although female birds lack this feature.

Immature male

Green-backed Woodpecker

Female

Female

Male

☐ **Grey-headed Bushshrike** 25 cm | 10"

A stunning bird of wooded areas that hops and glides through the tree canopy in search
of a variety of prey, including small reptiles, large insects and, sometimes, young birds.
Despite its bright plumage, it can be difficult to locate – so it is well worth familiarizing
yourself with its unmistakable call, a drawn-out, mournful whistle "*pheeeeuuuu*",
although it can also be heard making a variety of clicking calls and eerie, rising whistles.
Generally secretive, every now and again one will put on a great show for you and be
seen gliding on spread olive-green wings from one tree or bush to another. If you are
this lucky, try to observe how other birds react to it – most will avoid contact with this
glamorous but stealthy predator. The similar Sulphur-breasted Bushshrike (*not shown*)
is also found in the Serengeti, especially among acacias, but is smaller, shows a patch
of yellow above the eye leading down to the top of the bill, and sings a sweet, whistled
"*phew-pu-pu-pu-puuuuuu*".

▼

This species is sometimes confused with the male Village Weaver (*page 160*) which is also yellow with a black head so check if you are unsure of your identification.

☐ Tropical Boubou 21 cm | 8¼"

An easy-to-find bushshrike of open woodland and lodge gardens. At first glance, it appears all-white below and black above, including the eye, with a white bar running across the wing. Given close views, the underparts will be seen to have a peachy flush. There is a chance of confusion with the male Black-backed Puffback (*page 137*), which shares the same habitat – but the puffback is much smaller and has a red eye. As with most bushshrikes, one feature of their behaviour is synchronized calling, known as an antiphonal system. This involves one bird starting the duet with a series of notes and the other bird coming in seamlessly to finish the harmony. Until you see this for yourself, you may find it hard to believe that it is not a single bird making the call, but in fact two. In the case of the Tropical Boubou, "*poo-poo*" by the male is followed immediately by "*wey-hoo*" from the female. You are just as likely to encounter the antiphonal phenomenon with Slate-coloured Boubou (*page 141*) and the puffback.

▲ ☐ Black-headed Oriole
21 cm | 8¼"

A bright-yellow bird of open woodlands. As the name indicates, this bird shows a completely black head, although its bill is bright red. The back can show a hint of green and the central tail feathers are also rich olive-green. The flight feathers are mostly black but edged in white with a small white patch at the base. As with so many woodland birds, getting to know their calls is a great help when trying to locate them – so listen out for the oriole's strong, fluty "*weeeooo*" or descending "*weeo-weeoo*". Two other species of oriole can sometimes be seen in the Serengeti – Eurasian Golden Oriole and African Golden Oriole (*neither shown*) – but Black-headed is by far the most commonly encountered and the only one with a black head.

☐ Brown-throated Wattle-eye
13 cm | 5″

A small, pied bird of woodland and gardens. As their name suggests, both sexes show a distinctive bright-red, fleshy wattle above the eye that contrasts with the otherwise black head. Males show a white throat and black chest-band, while females have a maroon-coloured throat. Both sexes show a white flash in the wing and the back is black (rather than grey, as in the Chin-spot Batis). Wattle-eyes typically prefer thicker woodland. Male birds tend to call first with a low, four-note whistle, translating to "*he likes bam-boo*"; the female replying with a bouncy retort "*she supplies him bam-boo*". It is most likely to be encountered in the western Serengeti.

Female

Male

☐ Chin-spot Batis 10 cm | 4″
A tiny black, white-and-grey bird of open woodland and scrub. Both sexes show a grey crown and back, yellow eyes and a broad, white line through the wing. Male birds have a thick black band across the chest, while females have a distinctive rusty-brown spot on the chin (hence the name) and a thinner breast-band of the same colour. If you see one bird of a pair, then the other will be nearby. These attractive birds have a distinctive "*pee....poo*" call, the latter note being much lower than the first, which is often accompanied by snappy and burry notes. Despite their flycatcher-like behaviour, both batises and wattle-eyes are more closely related to shrikes.

Male

Female

136

Male showing the 'puff' back

Female

Male

☐ **Black-backed Puffback**   17 cm | 6¾″ ▲

A heavily marked, black-and-white bushshrike of gardens and open scrub. Essentially quite similar in plumage to both the Brown-throated Wattle-eye and Chin-spot Batis, it is much larger and there is only a subtle difference between male and female. Males show a greater contrast between a white belly and black back, while females are browner-backed, greyer below and show a pale spot between the eye and the bill. Both sexes have a red eye. Their name derives from the male's impressive display in which he ruffs up his white rump feathers into a fluffy ball and calls loudly "*took-took-took*", sometimes flying around with his back still puffed-up. Males also emit various whipped "*tikweeoo*" notes.

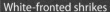

The family of true shrikes, which Includes the two fiscals shown here, are commonly known as 'butcherbirds' on account of their habit of impaling their prey, mostly invertebrates, on thorns and maintaining a 'larder' for harsher times. These are not to be confused with the true butcherbirds that are found in Australia.

Common Fiscal 23 cm | 9"

A common pied shrike of open bush, and the most widespread of the shrikes in the Serengeti and NCA. Common Fiscals are blackish above and white below with an obvious white bar across the upperwing when perched and in flight. The sexes look similar although females have a small chestnut patch on the flanks. It is frequently encountered perched in the open during game-drives that pass through bushy areas. Young birds are browner and heavily barred. The soft song is a sad melody of "*twee*" notes.

◀ ☐ Northern White-crowned Shrike 21 cm | 8¼"

A gregarious bird of dry scrub and low bush. Usually encountered in extended family groups, this distinctive shrike is very dark-backed and pale-fronted. The pattern of white crown, dark line through the eye and black cheeks is unique among shrikes in the region. When compared with the fiscal shrikes shown here, the Northern White-crowned Shrike is a much stockier bird with a shorter tail and shows an obvious white rump in flight. Young birds lack the white crown and are grubbier-looking. Social groups are noisy, giving a mix of nasal and chattering notes, including a Punch and Judy-like "*weer-haha*".

☐ Grey-backed Fiscal 25 cm | 10" ▼

A distinctive long-tailed shrike of open woodland and mixed scrub. The masked appearance of this bird, with grey crown, neck and back, are the best features for separating it from the Common Fiscal. Groups are sociable and engage in fits of tail-wagging while emitting squabbling calls from an exposed perch or sometimes from the ground. In flight, they appear very long-tailed and show a white flash in the wing and outer tail feathers.

☐ Common Drongo 25 cm | 10"

A black, fork-tailed bird usually seen
perched high in a tree or bush. Often
referred to as the Fork-tailed Drongo on
account of the deep 'V'-shaped notch in
the tail, adult birds have completely glossy
blue-black plumage and a red eye. Immature
birds are browner with black flecks in the
plumage. They appear more thickset than
the slimmer Northern Black Flycatcher,
especially around the neck, and show
a thicker, slightly hook-tipped bill.
The rambling call is a mix of
squawks and peeps. ▶

Drongos are insect hunters and
often sit in exposed positions
waiting for their quarry to fly by
before swooping onto their prey.
In flight, the lighter matt-brown
flight feathers contrast with the
black body and tail.

Juvenile

Adult

The Slate-coloured Boubou is a vocally versatile bird and, like the Tropical Boubou (*page 135*), has an antiphonal duet calling system. One call starts with a loud *"ch'shh-ch'shh"* followed by a woodblock-sounding *"coco-pop"*. Another series starts *"pa-ponk-pa-ponk"* followed by *"wee-eer"* and you might also hear several loud *"queerk-queerk"* notes returned with a low *"donk"*.

Slate-coloured Boubou 20 cm | 8"

A noisy, dark sooty-grey bird of low vegetation in bush and open woodland. It can appear all-black but a good view reveals a softer grey plumage especially on the back. Unlike the Common Drongo and Northern Black Flycatcher, this bird spends much of its time hopping on the ground or along low-lying branches and consequently has longer, sturdier legs. It rarely perches high in a tree so this should be a consideration when separating it from the other species shown here. A really useful identification feature for this bird is that the top of the bill obviously cuts upwards into the feathers of the forehead. In the other species shown here, the forehead feathers circle the top of the bill without interruption.

▲ ☐ Northern Black Flycatcher
18 cm | 7"

A slim, black bird that perches in the middle of trees and bushes. Frequently overlooked by birders and guides, this common matt-black flycatcher lives up to its name when swooping from its perch onto small flying invertebrates. Unlike the Common Drongo, it rarely sits out in the open, preferring to perch midway up a tree or bush with some cover, and is rarely seen on the ground. Young birds (*above right*) are heavily spotted with light-brown dots. It lacks the forked tail and pale flight feathers of the drongo and has dark rather than red eyes. The song is a soft, sweet refrain of quiet whistles and chips but it will sometimes mimic other species.

■ **Brown-crowned Tchagra** 19 cm | 7½" ▲

A secretive, streaky-headed bird of bush and rank grass. Pronounced 'chag-ra', this small, attractive bushshrike is common in suitable habitat across the Serengeti. As an indicator of habitat suitability, if there are Rattling Cisticolas (*page 148*) present you stand a good chance of finding this tchagra. The rich-chestnut wings help to separate both tchagras shown here from similar species, such as the Black-backed Puffback (*page 137*). Its call is a sweet, reverberating, descending whistle "*TIU-TIU-tiu-tiu-tiu*".

Black-crowned Tchagra 21 cm | 8"

Very similar to Brown-crowned Tchagra but, rather obviously, has an all-black crown. It is also a slightly larger bird and shows more contrast between the black eye-stripe and an otherwise white face. Another useful feature is the blue-grey colouration of the breast and belly, which is dirty white or buff in Brown-crowned Tchagra. The song is a beautiful whistled refrain that is quite unlike that of the Brown-crowned Tchagra

Common Bulbul 18 cm | 7" ▼

An abundant brown bird with a yellow vent. This is the most widespread of all East African birds and there are few places where it is not found. In the Serengeti, you are most likely to see it in the grounds of camps and lodges where it becomes very familiar and invades food halls and buffets with regularity. The common call is a downward "*he-wee-we-wer*", often accompanied with open, quivering wings.

Getting to know the Common Bulbul bird should be a priority, as it is the benchmark for reference when describing the size of many other songbirds.

▲ ☐ Spotted Morning Thrush
17 cm | 6½"

A heavily spotted rufous thrush of dry
and green thickets. Most common in the
dry areas, this rusty-brown songster is
quite approachable. It sings a beautifully
whistled song throughout the day between
bouts of feeding, when it often drops from
a low perch to collect morsels from the
ground. To the horror of many birders in
East Africa, this species has officially been
renamed as Spotted Palm Thrush simply
because it is a close relative of the Collared
Palm Thrush (*not shown*). However, the
Spotted is not fond of palms so most
prefer to call it by its more familiar name.

☐ Olive Thrush 22 cm | 8¾"

An uncommon garden bird with
a bright orange bill. Although it is
found in a select few lodge gardens in
the Serengeti, it is more likely to be
encountered at higher elevations in
the NCA where it is locally common.
This nondescript bird is usually seen
probing for worms on garden lawns in
the region, and fills the same ecological
niche as the American Robin or
European Blackbird (*neither shown*).
It likes to rest and hide away under
bushes, well away from the eyes of
dangerous avian predators. Young birds
are spotty on the breast and flanks.

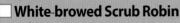

White-browed Scrub Robin
15 cm | 6"

A widespread songbird of dry scrub with a broad rufous tail and white in the wing. This spritely bird can look boring, brown and stripy one minute then brilliant the next – the difference all being down to the extraordinary tail which can be fanned wide open with dramatic effect. As with many other members of its family, these scrub robins are highly territorial and not only sing a great deal but will also engage in fighting with rivals, sometimes to the death!

Arrow-marked Babbler 22 cm | 8¾"

A medium-sized, dark-brown bird of bush and open woodland. This gregarious species lives in extended family groups and its noisy scowls leading into raucous disarray are usually the first sign of its presence. The many small, white chevrons down the throat and chest account for its name. Adult birds show bright-yellow eyes, while those of immatures are darker. Birds sift through leaf-litter, tossing it like a salad, looking for small invertebrates before flying a short distance on stiff wings to the next stop.

▲ □ White-eyed Slaty Flycatcher
15 cm | 6"

A blue-grey flycatcher with prominent white spectacles. Fairly common within its range, this flycatcher is most often encountered in well-wooded areas, especially those in the Crater Highlands. It tends to be less active than the other flycatchers, usually sitting quietly on an exposed perch waiting for prey to fly by and swooping to catch it in mid-air, but sometimes feeds by dropping to the ground. This bird is a soft blue-grey all-over with a slightly paler belly and obvious white eye-rings. Like the young of the Northern Black Flycatcher (*page 141*), the young of this species are heavily spotted with pale feathers but show the outline of an emerging white eye-ring. Its call is an agitated "*chrrrr-chrrrr*".

□ African Paradise Flycatcher
36 cm | 14"

A stunning chestnut and sooty-grey bird, sometimes with a very long tail. Despite its serene appearance, this is an aggressive, territorial bird that will often chase birds far larger than itself. They catch insects in swooping flights, often hovering before returning to rest on a perch to eat. Males in breeding plumage have an impressive long tail that can be at least three times the length of the head and body combined. Outside the breeding season, the tail streamers are lost and the males then look similar to female and immature birds. The amount of white in the wing depends on the local gene pool: some populations show none at all, whereas others show a large amount of white. Some birds lack any brown pigment and are completely white – although these are rare in the Serengeti and NCA and you will be very lucky to see one. The sharp contact call "*schwee-shurp*" sounds like the snapping of garden shears.

Male

Male
white
form

Female

Over a dozen species of cisticola have been recorded in the Serengeti and NCA, although only a few show distinctive colouration. They are difficult to identify and only the three commonest are included in this book: the Rattling Cisticola shown here and the Pectoral-patch and Zitting Cisticolas on *page 62*. The species are best separated by habitat preference and their unique calls, many of which are included in their common names, as is the case with Rattling Cisticola. Don't be too hard on yourself if they all look the same – it is best to concentrate on learning first the ones that you see and hear most often.

▢ Rattling Cisticola 14 cm | 5½"

The classic 'little brown job' (LBJ) of bush and scrub. This abundant small, brown warbler is heavily streaked above and pale below and has a relatively thick bill. It shows a brown crown that is lightly streaked but this is more chestnut in tone in immature birds. The tail is broad and rudder-like, edged with white spots that are evident in flight. Among the noisiest of small birds, it can often be heard shouting many harsh rasping notes that are followed by the rapid rattle *"chr-chr-chr-chr"*.

Red-faced Crombec

10 cm | 4"

A tiny bird with a very short tail. Its name does not help to describe the actual colour of this small bird, as the face and belly are cinnamon or dark-peach in tone, rather than red. The crown, back and wings are greyish-brown, as is the micro-short tail that may even appear to be absent. You will find it climbing and hopping through bushes and low trees, one after another, in search of food, and may hear its very high-pitched "*seeu*" call, although this can be difficult to trace.

Tawny-flanked Prinia

11 cm | 4¼"

A tiny brown bird with a long tail. Although appearing rather dull at first glance, the Tawny-flanked Prinia has a lot of personality for its size. It is often found in small, active groups and engage in frantic bouts of tail-swinging and calling – a zipping "*cheerp-cheerp*". Birds can be quite tame at times and a close approach will enable you to see the red eye and white eyebrow. The warm-brown flanks help to separate it from some other LBJs.

☐ Yellow-breasted Apalis ▲
13 cm | 5"

A long-tailed warbler with a lemon breast that often shows a black spot. The head is bluish-grey and the back and tail moss-green. A busy little bird of open bush and scrub, the Yellow-breasted Apalis is often found in pairs and has a unique song – one bird sings a rising "*ker-ker-keer-keer-keer*", while the other bird duets with a galloping horse-like "*territ-territ-territ*".

☐ Grey-backed Camaroptera
10 cm | 4"

A tiny grey-and-green warbler with a short tail. You stand a good chance of seeing this bird wherever there are trees with a rich understorey of vegetation. The grey head and back are complemented with moss-green wings. One feature you may observe when birds are hopping through the lower branches of dense vegetation is how white the feathers are under the tail. Birders will sometimes jest that it is called the 'camera-operator' because its call is similar to a camera with a whirring motor-drive shooting many frames "*di-der-der-der-der-der*". It can be quite approachable in the gardens of many of the camps and lodges in the Serengeti and NCA.

☐ Grey-capped Warbler 15 cm | 6" ▼

A vocal, green-backed warbler with a grey crown. This shy bird is frequently encountered wherever there is dark, damp and tangled vegetation, often near rivers and streams. It will sing loudly from the undergrowth – "*wuhu-chit-chit-chit-chit*" – but you may have to be patient for a bird to reveal itself. The grey crown contrasts with a narrow, black face-mask and, with a very good view, you may see a small, rusty-coloured bib.

General note: sunbirds are small, attractive nectar-feeders that are always 'on the go' and often attracted to flowers in lodge gardens. Males show bright, iridescent plumage, while females appear dowdy. When identifying these birds, pay particular attention to the size of the bird, the shape of its bill and the colour of the glossy sheen, which changes according to the light.

Female

☐ Scarlet-chested Sunbird
15 cm | 6"

A large, dark sunbird of woodland edge and gardens, with a long, decurved bill. Male birds have a spectacular red bib that is flecked with silvery-blue. In very good light they also show a green forehead, throat and moustache; the rest of the bird is black. Females are dark chocolate-brown with light streaking towards the vent. Immature males appear similar to females but are paler and show a hint of the red bib. The song is a rapid series of "*chip*" notes.

Male

☐ Collared Sunbird 10 cm | 4" ▼

A tiny, green-and-yellow sunbird. More restricted to woodland and forest than the other sunbirds shown here, the Collared is often seen feeding in trees rather than bushes and its diet includes more invertebrates. The sexes are quite similar – green above and lemon below – but males show an iridescent green breast underlined with a narrow, purple border. The song is less harsh than other sunbirds – a sweet, piercing "*see-yu*" repeated many times. The tiny nest is frequently raided by the brood-parasite Klaas's Cuckoo (*page 122*).

Female

Male

☐ Variable Sunbird ▶
11 cm | 4½"

A small sunbird of woodland and dry scrub. Female birds are dull grey-brown above and yellowish-green below, but the variety of colours in the male is a sight to behold. These are very busy birds that barely keep still – which doesn't help when you are trying to identify them! To separate the male from the similar but smaller Collared Sunbird, look for a blue or purple wash across the face and breast. You may also see a small orange feather or two between the wings and the breast – the pectoral tufts. The song is a series of rapid and rising "*chit-chit-chit-chit*" notes.

Male

Female

153

Marico Sunbird 12·5cm | 5" ▶

A small, dark and fast-moving sunbird. Given a good view in good light, males show a glossy-green head, back and upperwing, a black belly, and a conspicuous broad maroon band, bordered above with light blue, across the breast. Females are typically nondescript with an olive-brown back contrasting only slightly with buffy-olive underparts that are neatly spotted on the breast and belly but not the throat. Immature males are very similar to females but show a blackish throat. Where present, these sunbirds will attend multi-species flocks that gang-mob owls and other predators with repeated aggressive calls.

▼ **Beautiful Sunbird**   breeding male 15cm | 6"; female 8cm | 3½"

A very small and brilliantly coloured sunbird with a long tail that is commonly found in gardens and thorny scrub. Unlike the other long-tailed sunbirds shown here, breeding males are mostly iridescent green but show a bright orange-red breast-band bordered with yellow patches on the flanks. Most of the tail is black and fairly short but the central tail feathers are long and streamer-like. Females have a grey-brown head and back and are very pale and plain underneath, often cream-coloured but sometimes yellowish; immature males are similar but black-throated. Non-breeding males are similar to females but most show the long central tail streamers and a green patch on the shoulder. Both sexes are small-bodied and comparable in size to the Variable Sunbird (*page 153*). It is replaced by the larger Red-chested Sunbird (*page 202*) on the shores of Lake Victoria.

Male

Female

Non-breeding male

Male

Female

Bronze Sunbird breeding male 22 cm | 8¾"; female 12·5 cm | 5" ▼

A large, dark and long-tail sunbird with a strong bronze wash that is common in gardens and tangled scrub in the highlands. It is both noisy and conspicuous and among the easiest of the sunbirds to identify. Males appear dark but shine coppery-bronze in good sunlight and often have a greenish hue to the head and mantle. The underparts and tail are blackish and the central tail feathers are very long. Females show a strong yellow wash to their underparts and have a clean white throat and stripe over the eyes that contrast with the darker cheeks. The female's relatively short tail is dark brown, like the back, but shows white outer feathers. This bird sings a rambling chitter but you are much more likely to hear its piercing "*chu*" call notes.

Male

Female

Non-breeding male

White-browed Robin Chat 20 cm | 8″

A thrush-sized bird with a grey back and orange underparts. Common in lodge and camp gardens where there are large and scattered trees and lush undergrowth, the White-browed Robin Chat is generally a retiring bird, but can be easily tamed. With its striking head-pattern, bright underparts and burnt-orange tail in flight, this bird is easily recognised. The cyclical song starts quietly but increases in volume and pace. Pairs will often engage in powerful duets, especially when rival pairs are nearby, and the noise can be deafening. It is common to see this bird feeding its young, which are similar to the adults but heavily spotted and lack the strong face pattern. If you are very lucky, you may also see adults feeding a dark, heavily barred fledgling that is far larger than itself – this will be a juvenile Red-chested Cuckoo (*page 121*), a species that habitually lays its eggs in robin chat nests.

▼

Rüppell's Starling ▶
35 cm | 14″

A long-tailed, glossy starling with white eyes. Similar in general appearance to the Greater Blue-eared Starling, the Rüppell's Long-tailed Starling, as it used to be known, shows a long, graduated tail that befits the old name. Its obvious white eyes contrast with the matt-black head. The colouration of the body plumage varies between birds of different age and sex. Most show a deep-purple gloss with a green sheen to the wings, but some birds appear an iridescent cobalt-blue. They are highly vocal birds that sing a continuous, noisy chatter and whining, sometimes in the middle of the night; in flight their wings produce a whooshing sound.

These gaudy blue starlings are typically vocal but if you notice them becoming particularly noisy and agitated, it might be worth investigating further as they frequently harass predators, such as owls and birds of prey. Do proceed with caution, however, as they also mob dangerous snakes!

See under Rüppell's Vulture (*page 39*) to discover more about Rüppell.

Greater Blue-eared Starling ▶
23 cm | 9"

A large, glossy starling with orange-yellow eyes. This green-glossed starling shows a violet-blue sheen around the ears and belly in good light. Although often seen in trees, it tends to spend much of its time feeding on the ground and can be quite bullish in the company of other birds. The song is a jumbled mix of chittering warbles, but the call is easy to remember if you can imagine an old woman with a whining voice calling her husband Pat in for supper – "*pa-a-at*".

Look out for the nests of these birds in the tangle of old desert palm trees, which are often referred to as Balanites.

▼ ☐ **Superb Starling** 19 cm | 7½"

A common, multicoloured bird of open bush, plains and gardens. Often encountered in family groups, the Superb Starling lives up to its name with its 'coat of many colours'. When separating adults from the similar Hildebrandt's Starling, look for the obvious white line that divides the blue breast from the orange underparts, and the white eyes showing prominently in the black face. In flight it shows white under the wing and often calls a cheerful "*cheera-cherr-eet*".

Young Superb Starling can be separated from Hildebrandt's of the same age by their dark breast and white vent.

Adult

Juvenile

Superb Starling

Hildebrandt's Starling

Adult

Female

Male

Hildebrandt's Starling 19 cm | 7½"

A colourful, red-eyed starling of open woodland. Very similar in appearance to the Superb Starling, Hildebrandt's is more likely to be encountered in drier, wooded areas. It can be distinguished from Superb Starling by its red, rather than white, eyes and lack of a clean white line between the blue breast and orangey belly. The belly also tends to be more light-peach in colour than the bright orange of Superb Starling. In addition, its back tends to appear much darker blue and this colour extends to the shoulder; in Superb Starling the shoulders are green. In flight, it shows the same peach colour of the belly in the underwing, rather than white. The song comprises a series of slow-paced "*woo-wah*" notes mixed with chattering.

▲ Violet-backed Starling
17 cm | 6¾"

A small starling of open woodland. Unlike the other starlings in this book, the sexes are very different. Males show white underparts and a brilliant, iridescent, violet-coloured back, which accounts for its other names – Amethyst or Plum-coloured Starling. Females are light brown above and pale below but show dark streaking throughout. Flocks of these birds move with the seasons and the fruiting of trees, but often return to the same areas to breed in tree holes. In poor light, be careful as the glossy male can appear to be just black-and-white. It sings a series of quickly trilled notes.

Male

Female

Spectacled Weaver 14 cm | 5½″

An orange-faced, yellow weaver with pale-eyes. Often encountered in pairs in well-wooded areas, this unobtrusive weaver is aptly named on account of its narrow, black eye-mask. The face of both sexes has a warm glow and males also possess a black throat. Like the Baglafecht Weaver, this bird has a pointed, slender bill but shows a plain, moss-green coloured back. The call is often the first sign of its presence – a rapid, high-pitched, downward run of "*pipipipi*" notes.

Baglafecht Weaver 15 cm | 6″

A pale-eyed weaver with a black neck and cheeks. This distinctive bird is often found in pairs or small family groups. Males have black cheeks, neck and back, with fine yellow lines down the wings and tail. The similar females show an all-black crown and face. The bill is black, slender and pointed and the call is a buzzing, downward trill.

Male

Village Weaver 17 cm | 6¾″

A large, stout-billed, gregarious weaver with a red eye. Large colonies can often be found in acacia trees overhanging water. Breeding males are best identified by their black face that extends above the forehead, and the heavy black stripes running down the back. Females and non-breeding males lack the black face and heavy streaking on the back, instead showing greyish backs and a yellow throat and breast. The belly can be either white or yellow. The call comprises a series of repeated dry "*chip*" notes, while the song is a heady mix of wheezing and electronic-sounding "*whee*" notes. The most similar species is the Vitelline Masked Weaver of acacia country (*page 175*), but that bird is smaller and the breeding male lacks the black 'tramlines' down the back.

Male

Baglafecht Weavers do not nest in colonies and the untidy nest is often attached directly to a main branch rather than dangling down as in Village Weaver.

The woven nest of the **Village Weaver** hangs from a long 'stalk' and has an obvious bulbous chamber.

The nest of the **Spectacled Weaver** is very distinctive, having a long, tube-like entrance hanging from the side of the main chamber.

Spectacled Weaver
Juvenile

Baglafecht Weaver
Female

Village Weaver
Female

General note: Weavers are a large family of sparrow-sized birds that show great variation in their plumage. Most have varying amounts of yellow, with black in the face and body plumage. When identifying species, look out for the following features: face pattern; eye colour; bill size and shape; extent of markings on the back; nest shape; and social behaviour (*e.g.* whether it is in a flock).

Male

Female

☐ Purple Grenadier 13 cm | 5" ▲

A stunning purple-and-brown waxbill.
Widespread in dry bush and scrub,
although rarely seen in numbers, this
beautiful little bird shows a brown back,
violet-blue rump and dark tail in both
sexes. Males have patchy purple-blue
areas in the breast and belly, while females
show brown bars below. Both sexes
have decorative colouration around the
eyes – dark-blue in males but light-blue
and studded in females. It is often found
feeding near the base of bushes and
thickets, giving a soft, high-pitched call
"*tseet-tseet*" as it moves around – a sound
you may struggle to hear.

☐ Red-cheeked Cordon-bleu
13 cm | 5"

A delicate waxbill with bright-blue
underparts and light-brown back.
Frequent in open bush, gardens and
lightly wooded areas, you may also see
them in villages, often in pairs, mixing
with the Red-billed Firefinch (*page 180*).
The common call, a high-pitched "*peet-
pit-pit-pit*", is quite similar to that of the
firefinch. The sexes look similar, both
having pinkish bills and brown crowns,
but females lack the dark-red cheek-patch
of the male. They are a common host
to the Pin-tailed Whydah (*page 164*), a
brood-parasite of the waxbill family.

☐ **Bronze Mannikin** 9 cm | 3½"

A tiny, brown waxbill with a white belly.
Often occurring in small numbers in well-wooded
areas and gardens, these birds also gather in flocks to
feed on grass seeds at the woodland edge. The mostly
dark-brown plumage shows barring on the flanks, while
the shoulders have a dark green gloss in good light.
The bill is short and stout, typical of granivorous (seed-
eating) birds. It is most frequently heard in flight, when
the short, buzzing "*pee-pu*" call catches the attention.

The three species
shown here belong
to the waxbill or
Estrildid family.
Although they do not
possess 'waxbill' in
their common names,
they are related to
the Common Waxbill
(*page 102*).

▼

Female

Male

163

Male

Female

■ Pin-tailed Whydah

breeding male 30 cm | 12"; female 10 cm | 4"

Small, seed-eating birds with a variety of plumages. Breeding males display impressive long tail-streamers which they dangle in a hanging flight (*above*) over the drab brown females while calling continuously "*tsweet-tsweet-tsweet*". Non-breeding males look similar to the stripe-headed females but retain a red bill and have more white in the face. They are closely related to the Village Indigobird (*page 180*) and, like that species, are a brood-parasite of the waxbill family. However, unlike cuckoos and many other brood-parasites, whydahs and indigobirds do not evict the eggs of the host family and their chicks grow up with the rest of the brood.

Golden-breasted Bunting 15 cm | 6"

An attractive bird with a golden-yellow breast and a striped head. These birds are widespread in the Serengeti and NCA where there is open woodland and scrub. They are shy and often take flight when disturbed from the ground (where they feed), but often just into a nearby tree or bush allowing close inspection. Given good views you will see a mix of black and white stripes on the head and two white bars in the wings. The mostly yellow breast has an orange hue that shines like gold in good light. They are most often encountered in pairs, never in flocks, and males sing their twittering song from an exposed perch high in a tree – a delightful "*tee-tu-tee-tu*" ending with a pronounced "*pee-chew*".

Yellow-fronted Canary 11 cm 4¼"

A yellow finch with a greenish, streaked back. This canary shows an all-yellow belly and dark-green stripes on the face. It is often found along woodland edges and in grassland with scattered bushes, unlike the similar White-bellied Canary (*page 173*) that is generally found in drier areas, especially where acacia scrub abounds. However, beware that the bright-yellow breast and eyebrow is common to both species. These close relatives will sometimes mix where habitats meet, so pay close attention to belly colour. Both canaries gather in small groups and show bright yellow rumps as they take off.

Red-and-yellow Barbet
22 cm | 8¾"

A brightly coloured barbet often associated with tall termite mounds in open savanna, especially in the NCA. There is no mistaking this charismatic bird of dry areas and family groups are a joy to watch. The white spots in the plumage are much larger and more conspicuous than those on the duller Usambiro Barbet (*page 128*), which also lacks the red in the face and red bill. They feed on a mixed diet of seeds and invertebrates and both nest and roost in termite mounds, a dominant pair often having sibling or offspring helpers. Pairs proclaim their territory with a ritualized duet that translates to a rambling "*red'n'yellow, red'n'yellow....*"

Red-fronted Barbet
17 cm | 6½"

A common but inconspicuous barbet of lightly wooded acacia scrub. This medium-sized barbet is easily identified if the white throat and distinctive face pattern are seen. The red front to the crown is not always easy to see and is a feature that is shared with the much smaller Red-fronted Tinkerbird (*page 129*). However, the tinkerbird lacks the thick black line through the face. Red-fronted Barbets nest in tree holes and are frequent victims of the honeyguides (*page 130*), which are brood-parasites.

White-bellied Go-away-bird 50 cm | 20"

A large grey bird with a tall crest and long tail.
Like the Bare-faced Go-away-bird (*page 120*),
this go-away-bird does not scream "*Go Away*"
but calls "*WAH*" very loudly and runs along
the branches of trees in great excitement, often
hopping from one to the next. The white belly
is obvious when the underside is seen and in
flight the bird shows distinctive white bands
against the darker wings and tail. This bird is
far more abundant east of the Great Rift Valley
but has recently become established in the
dry south of the Serengeti and in the NCA.

▼ ☐ Blue-naped Mousebird 35 cm | 14"

A small grey bird with a long tail. Very similar in size and shape to the Speckled Mousebird (*page 117*), the Blue-naped Mousebird prefers drier, open habitats and is particularly fond of acacia scrub. Its plumage is mostly grey, rather than brown as in Speckled Mousebird, the cheeks are plain (rather than white), and it has a red eye-patch extending to the base of the bill. It also shows a more pronounced, stiff crest which adds to its elegant appearance. Listen out for the distinctive high-pitched "*peeu-peeu-peeu*" call when in flight, which is rapid and direct rather than clumsy and weak as in Speckled Mousebird.

☐ Abyssinian Scimitarbill
24 cm | 9½"

A slender black bird with a long, strongly decurved bill, which is orange in adults and dark in young birds. Very similar in appearance to the Common Scimitarbill (*page 127*), the Abyssinian favours much drier and open habitats, especially acacia scrub. A diagnostic feature is the lack of any white bars or spots in the wings and tail, which is obvious during its floppy flight, In good light, look for a violet sheen to the upperparts. It is often seen hanging on small tree trunks and branches probing for invertebrates. Listen for its descending "*kree-kree-kree*" call.

◀

Male

Female

Named after Baron Carl Claus von der Decken (1833–1865), a German explorer who was the first European to attempt a Kilimanjaro summit climb. He failed.

☐ Von der Decken's Hornbill   48 cm | 19"   ▲

A black-backed hornbill with a red or black bill. These birds are slow-moving and rather clumsy inhabitants of acacia thicket, where they feed on a variety of fruits, invertebrates and small reptiles. Males have a bright-red bill with a yellow tip, while the bill of the females is black. Unlike other small hornbills found in Tanzania, this bird shows an unspotted back in both sexes and two large white wing-panels, most obvious during its undulating flight. Its call is a low, unassuming "*kuk-kuk-kuk-kuk*". Like the African Grey Hornbill (*page 119*), this species seals the entrance to the nest hole to deter predators and nest-site rivals, the imprisoned female incubating the eggs and raising the young while being fed through a small opening by the male.

The name of this shrike derives from the Wataita people who settled in what is now known as the Taita-Taveta region of southern Kenya.

☐ **Taita Fiscal** 20cm | 8"

A small grey-backed shrike with a black cap. This is a close relative to the Grey-backed and Common Fiscals (*pages 138–139*) and shares features of both species (*i.e.* the black cap of a Common Fiscal and the grey back of the Grey-backed Fiscal). However, this bird has a shorter tail than both of these species and is restricted to dry acacia scrub, where it is thinly distributed. The sexes are similar but females show a small chestnut smudge on the flanks that may be tricky to see in the field.

☐ **Brubru** 14cm | 5½"

A peculiar-looking bushshrike with a distinctive voice. This bird of dry scrub could be confused with a variety of other similar-looking species, including the tchagras (*page 142*), but the Brubru is short-tailed and very white in the face and breast. The crown, back and wings are blackish in males and brown in females and both show off-white lines through the face, neck and wings. Also look out for the bright-chestnut flanks. The song is a distinctive rolling trill, "*prrrrrrrp-prrrrrrrrp*", not dissimilar to an old telephone ringing, which is far-carrying.

Magpie Shrike 43 cm | 17" ▼

A long-tailed, black bird with distinctive white shoulders.
Often encountered in loose family groups, the Magpie Shrike is typical of its family as
it tends to perch still for several minutes before dropping onto its prey, which consists
mostly of insects and other invertebrates. It moves between trees with a weak, fluttery
flight, when the white shoulder patches and white rump are obvious. It is unlikely to be
confused with other shrikes as it is the only one with a black belly, but compare with
other long-tailed, dark birds such as Ruppell's Starling (*page 156*), Green Wood-hoopoe
(*page 127*) and Common Scimitarbill (*page 127*), all of which lack the white shoulders.

◀ ■ Silverbird 18 cm | 7"

An attractive silver-grey flycatcher with orange underparts. The distinctive plumage makes the adults unmistakable given a good view, but immature birds are more difficult to identify as they are brown and lightly spotted with buff and black. It is likely to be encountered only in open acacia scrub, which is patchily distributed in the Serengeti, but is widespread at lower elevations within the NCA, where pairs are common. Like many flycatchers, it sits and waits for its prey to fly by. They are shy and as they rarely allow a close approach you are unlikely to hear the sweet whistled "*cheet-siri-EET-weet*" song.

◀ ■ African Grey Flycatcher 14 cm | 5½"

A small, grey bird with a lightly streaked crown. It shows a rather large head for its body size, the black eye and plain face giving it a rather 'beady-eyed' appearance. Often found sitting upright on the outer branches of an acacia or other small bush in the dry belt, this rather plain flycatcher is usually found in small, loose parties. Rather than taking flies on the wing, as with the African Paradise Flycatcher (*page 146*), this bird generally drops to the ground for its quarry. You are more likely to hear its "*shree-shree*" alarm call than its simple song.

White-bellied Canary 11 cm | 4½"

A yellow, lightly streaked finch with a white belly. Very similar to the Yellow-fronted Canary (*page 165*), the White-bellied Canary prefers drier country with acacia scrub, although sometimes the species mingle where habitats meet. It is a seed-eater that feeds mostly on the ground and always shows a white belly and less heavily marked facial streaking than the Yellow-fronted Canary. It is not shy and is often present in and around Maasai villages.

Foxy Lark 16 cm | 6½"

A streaky, brown lark with a broad white eye-brow. This lark is common in the dry zone where it is often found singing its rambling scratchy song from the top of a small acacia. It is smaller and slimmer than the chunky Rufous-naped Lark (*page 63*), has a thinner bill and appears more stripy. It has a chestnut flash in the open wing and often shows chestnut tones on the crown and cheeks, although this is quite variable. This species was formerly known as Fawn-coloured Lark in East Africa.

The nest of the Grey-capped Social Weaver is an untidy bundle of dry grasses, often on the outermost branches of a Whistling Thorn acacia, and sometimes shows a prominent entrance hole. Occasionally, pairs will combine nests making a double- or even treble-sized nest that is shared.

☐ Grey-capped Social Weaver
11 cm | 4½"

A very small, brown weaver likely to be found in large colonies in the dry lands. A busy colony may exceed 100 birds and you are likely to find them by hearing their busy calls, a series of "*chew-chew-chew*" notes. Obvious identification features include the creamy-grey cap and the very short tail that has a whitish tip. Note that the plumage is quite unlike that of any of the other weavers or sparrows in the Serengeti and NCA.

▼ ☐ Speckle-fronted Weaver
11 cm | 4½"

A small, sparrow-like weaver that is common in barren areas of acacia scrub and also sometimes around the outskirts of villages. It is best identified by the chestnut-brown patch at the back of the neck, but also look for the speckled forehead, although this can often be difficult to see. It has a pale face and appears rather beady-eyed, setting it apart from other small birds in the same flock. The nest tends to be more hidden than those of most other weavers, often being situated low down in an acacia rather than hanging from the end of a branch.

Check out the similar sparrows on *pages 178–179*.

The nest of the Vitelline Masked Weaver is very easy to identify as it is always onion-shaped and rarely shows an entrance tube.

Male

▢ Vitelline Masked Weaver
13 cm | 5″

A common weaver that is at home around villages in the dry acacia belt. It is similar to the larger Village Weaver (*page 160*) but can be easily separated given a good view. Although both species have red eyes and a warm chestnut border to their black face-mask, the black on the male Vitelline Weaver's head does not extend onto the crown or down onto the breast, and its back does not have strong black 'tramlines' as in Village Weaver. The female Vitelline Weaver has a pale, narrow bill compared to the dark, heavy bill of the female Village Weaver, and the breast and flanks are generally a warm buff contrasting with the white belly.

Female

Check out the similar weavers on
pages 160–161 **and** *203–205*.

Red-billed Buffalo Weaver
22 cm | 8¾"

A large and dark weaver with a red bill. Males are essentially black all-over but often show a scruffy white patch near the shoulder and a sharp, red bill. Females and immatures are dark brown with a red or pink bill. Like the other large weavers covered here, this species feeds on seeds gleaned from the ground and is often located when flocks fly up to an acacia. The nest is huge, often exceeding one metre in length, and is built mostly from thorny twigs with virtually no grass; several nests are often built in one tree, often an acacia.

White-headed Buffalo Weaver
18 cm | 7"

An unmistakable large weaver with a white head and underparts, dark back and a bright-red rump. This bird is easy to find in the dry bush of the north as it often gathers in open trees and shrubs along roadsides. It is a colonial bird but the nests are well dispersed across a wide area so there may only be one or two nests per tree. The nest itself is very large in relation to the size of the bird and is typically more twiggy than that of the Vitelline Masked Weaver (*page 175*), for example. Look out for the white wing patches when the bird is in flight and listen out for the loud, parrot-like "*cheeya*" calls.

Rufous-tailed Weaver 22 cm | 8¾"

A large and scruffy brown weaver with a rufous tail. This species has a very small global distribution and breeds only in this north-west corner of Tanzania and, since 2010, across the border in the Masai Mara. However, it is common in the Serengeti and NCA, where it nests in colonies, often with other weavers and sparrows. Adults are scaly-looking with a dark bill and blue eyes, while young birds are dark-eyed and have a yellow bill. This species spends long periods on the ground searching for seeds and can be overlooked but is often easy to find in the Ngorongoro Crater where it attends picnic tables for scraps.

The nest of the Rufous-tailed Weaver is a particularly untidy globe of long straws of dry grass and twigs, usually in an acacia.

The technical term for seed-eating birds is granivorous.

Swahili Sparrow ▶
15 cm | 6"

The common 'grey-headed' sparrow in the Serengeti and NCA. The Swahili Sparrow has the smallest bill of the variable Grey-headed Sparrow complex of species. It is a gentle-looking sparrow that, like the other sparrows shown here, is very much at home in the company of people, feeding primarily on the ground. The white bar in the wing is not always easy to see but watch out for the chestnut-coloured rump that is obvious in flight. Its calls are quite unmusical, mostly dry "*chips*" and not much else.

Kenya Rufous Sparrow ▶
14 cm | 5½"

The native equivalent of the House Sparrow that is common in and around large hotels and tented camps. Both sexes can easily be told from House Sparrow by their white eyes, and males have grey rather than white cheeks. Although females lack the 'sparkle' of the males, they are still more colourful than female House Sparrows and often show chestnut on the back and warm tones to the face.

Male

Female

■ House Sparrow 14 cm | 5½"

A common species that will probably be familiar to visitors from most parts of the world. The House Sparrow was introduced to the coast of East Africa around 100 years ago but has since spread westwards to the Serengeti and is now a regular in Maasai bomas and villages in the east of the reserve and the NCA. Males show a distinctive head-pattern: white cheeks; a large, black throat-patch bleeding into the top of the breast; a grey crown; and dark-chestnut at the back of the neck. Females are very bland, lacking much in the way of colour. Both sexes have dark eyes, unlike the Kenya Rufous Sparrow, adults of which have white eyes. House Sparrows give a classic, monotonous chirping call.

Male

Female

The House Sparrow is one of the most successful bird species in the world and occurs on all continents apart from Antarctica. Although it is an introduced species in East Africa, it is quite passive and does not appear to pose a threat to any of the native species.

The nests of all three species shown here are generally more secluded than in the closely related weavers, often being built in the thatched roof of a building or a tree hole.

Male

Female

Male

Female

Red-billed Firefinch 10 cm | 4"

A tiny, red-and-brown waxbill. These are common ground-feeders that associate with sparrows and doves in villages of the NCA, often in flocks of 20 or more, but may also be found in leafy gardens. Males are deep-red, like a fine claret, with a red-and-grey bill. The back is brown and you may be able to see many tiny white dots around the breast area. Females are light brown all-over, have a distinctive red rump and typically show brighter white spots on the underparts than males. This firefinch frequently associates with the Village Indigobird, which is a brood-parasite dependent upon this species. The rarely encountered African Firefinch (*not shown*) is similar, but birds of both sexes show a black vent and a silver-blue bill.

Village Indigobird 10 cm | 4"

A tiny black bird with a white bill and pink legs. Usually found in close association with the Red-billed Firefinch, male indigobirds are easy to pick out in the crowd. Females are slightly trickier due to their drab brown plumage but can be separated from the very similar female Pin-tailed Whydah (*page 164*) by their plain breast that lacks any stripes. Village Indigobirds are part of the whydah family, which are brood-parasites, and specialize in laying their eggs in the nests of Red-billed Firefinch. Strangely, the host does not seem to mind sharing its home with the indigobird and the young grow up with a healthy bond.

☐ **Pied Crow** 46 cm | 18"

A large, black bird with a white breast and neck. Like many other crows around the world, this is a clever opportunist that forages around towns and villages in search of food. It will often steal food from other birds and animals, and may then store the bounty for leaner times. The larger, but otherwise similar, White-necked Raven (*page 182*) can easily be separated from the Pied Crow at a distance by its black breast and smaller white patch at the back of the neck. Also, the bill of this crow is not as heavy as that of the raven. The gruff "*caar-caar*" notes are typically crow-like.

Crows are capable of complex problem-solving and one of the few bird families that have a proven ability to count.

Schalow's Turaco 40 cm | 16"

Secretive but brightly plumaged birds of highland forests and riverine woodland. Given the incredible colouration of these birds, it is perhaps rather surprising that they are usually heard before they are seen. The call is a series of up to ten raucous "*caw*" notes that rises in volume and intensity for the first five notes before subsiding. This is usually repeated every thirty seconds or so. The first glimpse of this bird is usually as it glides from one tree to the next on bright-red wings that contrast with the bright-green body and blue tail. A close view of the face reveals even more beauty – a red ring around the eye with a short white line in front and a longer white line below; and a long, green crest with each feather tipped in white.

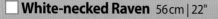

The green colour in the turaco's plumage comes from the pigment turacoverdin, and the red colour in the wings from the pigment turacin, both of which are unique to turaco species. In other birds, these colours are produced from carotenoids.

White-necked Raven 56 cm | 22"

A huge crow with a white neck. In the Serengeti and NCA, this crow can only be confused with the Pied Crow (*page 181*) but that species shows an obvious white breast. The white-tipped bill of the raven is massive, rather grotesque even, but is very practical for tearing at carcasses. However, nowadays it is more likely to be found scavenging at picnic sites in the crater, and sometimes near villages at lower elevations, than feeding on carcasses.

▲
☐ **Crowned Hornbill** 55 cm | 21½"

A brown hornbill with a red bill and pale eyes. This woodland-dwelling hornbill is not uncommon on the forested slopes of the Ngorongoro Crater and is often located by its call, a high-pitched series of "*pew*" notes. It feeds in the tree canopy on a variety of fruits and large invertebrates such as grasshoppers, and may also tackle chameleons and other lizards. It shows no white in the wing in flight but the white belly is conspicuous if seen well.

183

Cinnamon-chested Bee-eater
22 cm | 8¾"

A green-backed bee-eater with a yellow throat and dark cinnamon underparts. This species is very similar to Little Bee-eater (*page 123*) but is larger, much darker below and does not show a narrow blue line above the black eye-mask (a good identification feature of Little Bee-eater). Despite their physical similarities, habitat preference is probably the best way to separate the two with this species requiring good stands of mature trees in well-wooded areas from where they dart after their airborne insect prey.

African Stonechat
13 cm | 5"

A dainty little bird of highland scrub. Often found perched prominently on bushes and ferns on the crater rim, this small chat often drops to the ground before darting back to a perch. Compared to the rather drab females, the boldly marked male birds are easier to find but pairs form tight bonds and are usually very close. In flight, they both show a white rump and a flash of white in the wing.

☐ Streaky Seedeater 14cm | 5½" ▼

A heavily streaked brown finch of bushy areas. The sexes are similar in this plain-looking species that lacks any bright colours in its plumage. The streaking extends from under the white throat all the way to the tail and it shows a strongly marked face. Compared to canaries and buntings, which often stand with their bellies very close to the ground, it appears more 'leggy' than both and hops with its belly well off the ground.

Female

Male

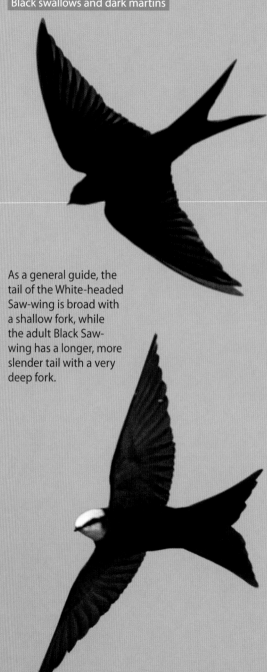

Black Saw-wing
15 cm | 6"

An all-black swallow with a forked tail. Seen well in good light, it obviously lacks the white head of the White-headed Saw-wing, but is otherwise very similar. The best identification feature is the long tail which shows a very deep fork. The plumage is blacker than the dark chocolate-brown of White-headed Saw-wing, although this can be difficult to determine when birds are flying and appear in silhouette. The Black Saw-wing is rarely found away from forest, and is most often seen flying around the trees on the Ngorongoro Crater rim.

As a general guide, the tail of the White-headed Saw-wing is broad with a shallow fork, while the adult Black Saw-wing has a longer, more slender tail with a very deep fork.

White-headed Saw-wing
14 cm | 5½"

A smart, dark-brown swallow with a white head. These delightful little birds breed in the sandy banks of rivers usually where there is a tangle of tree roots to conceal the nest hole. Although they are most frequently found along the edges of riverine forest, they are sometimes seen over the open plains. Adult males have a crisp, white cap and chin, giving them a very distinctive appearance, while females typically only show a pale chin. Immatures lack the white head markings and are almost impossible to separate from immature Black Saw-wings. Both saw-wing species give a simple, drawn-out "*chew*" call with some random chattering.

◀ ☐ **Plain Martin** 12 cm | 4¾"

A brown martin of riverine habitats. Also known as the Brown-throated or African Sand Martin, this bird is very common along the Mara and Grumeti rivers. It is mostly sandy-brown all-over but has a whitish belly and a dark, grey-brown throat. It excavates nest holes in sandy river banks, and colonies are easily found. Other bird species, including swifts, swallows and other martins, frequently take over the nest holes.

☐ **Banded Martin** 15 cm | 6" ▶

A large, brown martin with a broad chest-band. Unlike the Plain Martin, this charming bird shows a clean white throat and belly, and a close view reveals a white comma-shaped marking in front of the eye. It could be mistaken for the smaller Sand Martin (*not shown*), a migrant from Europe, which lacks the white 'eye comma', and both are frequently seen over marshes and grassland.

☐ Mosque Swallow 21 cm | 8"

A large blue-capped swallow with a red rump and orange under the tail. Less numerous than the other resident swallows shown here, the Mosque Swallow has never really shown a preference for Muslim places of worship but prefers old trees with suitable nest-holes instead. When flying overhead, look out for the white underwing contrasting heavily with the dark flight feathers.

☐ Red-rumped Swallow
18 cm | 7"

A blue-capped swallow with a red rump and black under the tail. It breeds mostly in or near to buildings and shows orange cheeks compared to the white cheeks of the larger Mosque Swallow but is otherwise very similar.

☐ Rufous-chested Swallow
20 cm | 8"
A blue-capped swallow with blue cheeks and warm, reddish underparts. This swallow is scarce on the Serengeti and NCA grasslands but small numbers breed, unusually, in the disused subterranean burrows of creatures like Aardvark. Like the other blue-backed species shown here, it shows a red rump in flight.

☐ Lesser Striped Swallow 17 cm | 6¾"
A chestnut-headed swallow with a red rump and heavily striped underparts. It is a common resident with a preference for riverine habitats, where it frequently nests under bridges. These attractive birds will also nest in camps and lodges wherever an overhang provides shelter, such as under the fly-sheets of tents or the eaves of lodge roofs.

189

Wire-tailed Swallow

☐ **Wire-tailed Swallow** 18 cm | 7"

A blue-backed swallow with a chestnut cap and white underparts. This is a widespread resident of the Serengeti and NCA, occurring almost everywhere. It frequently breeds close to water, including under bridges, and may also be found nesting in outbuildings, especially at airstrips. The end of the tail is straight, not forked, and, in most plumages, shows two prominent stiff and straight outer tail feathers. By far the best identification feature is the clean white throat and belly, which separates it from other blue-backed swallows.

☐ **Angola Swallow** 15 cm | 6"

A common resident swallow of the western Serengeti and Speke Bay area that is most similar to the Barn Swallow. Unlike that species, which shows a red throat and dark-blue breast-band, the Angola Swallow has an extensive reddish throat that extends over the upper breast. Barn Swallows are typically white or cream on the underparts but Angola Swallows appear dusky-grey on the underparts, both in flight and when perched. Another useful field feature of Angola Swallow is the neatly forked tail that never shows long tail streamers, a useful characteristic of adult Barn Swallows. Although this species is not a classic migrant, it is known to travel as far as the Rift Valley from Lake Victoria and could therefore turn up almost anywhere.

Angola Swallow

Barn Swallow

Barn Swallow 19 cm | 7½"

A blue-backed swallow with a red throat and pale belly. Familiar to many visitors from outside of Tanzania, the Barn Swallow is among the most cosmopolitan of all bird species. It is a common migrant to the Serengeti and NCA between September and April, but stragglers have been recorded in all months of the year. In flight, it appears glossy-blue above and white or cream-coloured on the belly. When perched, good views of the velvet-red throat and blue breast-band help to separate it from the Angola Swallow, which is a less frequent visitor to the plains. Young Barn Swallows are less strongly marked than adults and lack the long tail streamers of birds in breeding plumage (as do many adults that arrive into Tanzania from September onwards).

◀ ☐ **Little Swift** 14cm | 5½"

One of two common swifts in the Serengeti and NCA that show a white rump and white throat. The Little Swift is best separated from the White-rumped Swift by its short, square-ended tail, which spreads into a rounded fan as it banks. It is very common around villages where it often forms large, chittering flocks overhead. Birds range widely across plains to feed and are often seen over rivers and marshes. It regularly breeds in solid buildings and makes its nest from feathers and its own saliva. During display, this swift will often find a feather and fly with it in its bill as an invitation to others that it is ready to mate.

◀ ☐ **White-rumped Swift** 15cm | 6"

The other common swift with a white rump that is regularly seen over the villages, plains and marshes of the Serengeti and NCA. It is separated from the Little Swift by its much longer, forked tail, although in level flight the fork is not always visible and the tail looks long and pointed. To be sure of your identification, just wait a while until the bird banks and spreads its tail. Another feature to look out for is a thin white line along the rear edge of the upperwing – known as the 'trailing edge' – which is lacking in Little Swift. As in that species, and given a close view, you may also notice a clean white throat on this bird. White-rumped Swifts will often breed under bridges, with or without water running underneath, and may make excited trilling sounds as they return to the nest.

◀ ☐ African Palm Swift 18 cm | 7"

A uniform, light-brown swift with a long, pointed tail. As its name suggests, this resident species is dependent upon palm trees for nesting and it can often be found hawking for insects in their vicinity. It is common wherever palms are abundant. The long tail often appears fused at the tip but when banking in the air, it is frequently spread to reveal a deep notch.

☐ Nyanza Swift 17 cm | 6¾" ▶

A dark-brown swift with pale wing-panels. This species appears very similar to the Common Swift but in the fast, active flight, the pale patches on the wings can usually be seen – both from above and below. It is worth noting, however, that the Nyanza Swift is resident in East Africa (breeding mostly in the Rift Valley), and so can be seen year-around in the Serengeti and NCA (not just between October and April as with Common Swift). It is often seen singly or in small numbers rather than vast flocks. Its call is a trill rather than a scream, but birds tend not to be very vocal in the Serengeti.

☐ Common Swift 18 cm | 7" ▶

A dark-brown swift with a lightly forked tail. A common migrant from Europe and Asia between October and April, the Common (or Eurasian) Swift often arrives ahead of big storms and in huge numbers. Loose flocks can number in excess of 10,000 birds and may take hours to pass overhead – a great example of bird migration that you can actually sit back, admire and enjoy! Like other swifts, they fly very quickly, so getting a good view requires some dexterity with your binoculars. They are generally silent when wintering in Africa, but if you are from Europe or Asia, you may be familiar with their high-pitched screams that herald the arrival of the northern summer.

☐ Eurasian Bee-eater 28 cm | 11"

A stunning migrant from Europe that is often seen
migrating overhead in sizeable flocks. Birds typically
appear on their southward journey between the end of
September and early November, and then again heading
north in March and April, although small numbers
are suspected to spend the winter in some parts of
the Serengeti and NCA. Listen for their soft, churring
"*prruut-prruut*" calls as they drift leisurely overhead,
and enjoy watching them make dashing flights after
bees, wasps and dragonflies.

Eurasian Bee-eater

☐ Blue-cheeked Bee-eater 30 cm | 12"

A brilliant-green bee-eater with a long, pointed tail.
Often seen perched in open bush, and frequently near
water, this stunner shows a rich rufous colouration to
the underwing in flight. It is a migrant from the Near
East, arriving in October and departing around April,
while the similar Madagascar Bee-eater (*not shown*),
which sports a rusty-brown cap and has less blue in the
face, visits the region from May to September. The calls
of both species are a series of trilled "*preep*" notes.

Blue-cheeked Bee-eater

☐ White-throated Bee-eater 28 cm | 11"

A colourful bee-eater with a black collar and cap. As
the name suggests, this beauty shows an obvious white
throat in all plumages but only the adults have the long
central tail-streamers. During any encounter with this
bird, look out for the kaleidoscope of colours and long
bill. It breeds in small numbers around Lake Natron but
most birds seen in the region will be migrants from dry
areas of Africa south of the Sahara.

White-throated Bee-eater

These three species are among the most stunning birds to grace the skies of the Serengeti
and NCA but, sadly, none of them are resident in the area covered in this guide. As explained
in their species accounts above, they are all migrants from further afield. The White-throated
Bee-eater breeds in the lower Rift Valley, just 100 km north-east of the Ngorongoro Crater, but
remains an irregular visitor throughout the year with a peak in observations occurring between
December and May. The other two species are longer-distance migrants and are only likely to
be encountered between September and April. Because of their wandering habits, all three
are mostly encountered in the air, where they take advantage of local insect populations with
amazing grace and agility. If you are fortunate enough to see any of these species perched,
perhaps resting during migration, take full advantage and consider it a very special sighting.

◼ Pearl-spotted Owlet 19 cm | 7½"

A tiny, spotted owl of open scrub and wooded savannah. Despite its small size, not much bigger than a sparrow, this fearsome little predator regularly takes small birds and sometimes small mammals and reptiles, as well as large invertebrates. It is primarily nocturnal but can also be active during the day. The large, bright-yellow eyes glare and you may also notice the neat pair of white eyebrows. On the back of the head is a pair of black 'false eyes' which may intimidate predators. The chest is streaked with chestnut-brown and the bird gets its name from the numerous small, creamy spots on its back. The commonest call is a continuous piped "*peu-peu-peu*" that rises to a crescendo and finishes with long whistles. This is a useful call to learn, since many small birds are attracted to it and will mob the dangerous owl.

Grey form

Brown form

African Scops Owl

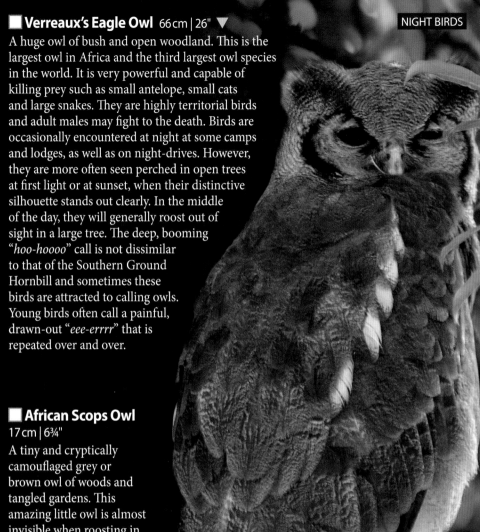

■ Verreaux's Eagle Owl 66 cm | 26" ▼

A huge owl of bush and open woodland. This is the largest owl in Africa and the third largest owl species in the world. It is very powerful and capable of killing prey such as small antelope, small cats and large snakes. They are highly territorial birds and adult males may fight to the death. Birds are occasionally encountered at night at some camps and lodges, as well as on night-drives. However, they are more often seen perched in open trees at first light or at sunset, when their distinctive silhouette stands out clearly. In the middle of the day, they will generally roost out of sight in a large tree. The deep, booming "*hoo-hoooo*" call is not dissimilar to that of the Southern Ground Hornbill and sometimes these birds are attracted to calling owls. Young birds often call a painful, drawn-out "*eee-errrr*" that is repeated over and over.

■ African Scops Owl
17 cm | 6¾"

A tiny and cryptically camouflaged grey or brown owl of woods and tangled gardens. This amazing little owl is almost invisible when roosting in trees by day and you may need an expert guide to show you one. The best way to find one by yourself is to imitate the call very early in the morning and follow the reply. That call is a simple purred whistle "*prruu*", which is repeated every five seconds or so. This owl feeds mostly on insects and amphibians.

Named after the French bird specimen collector J. P. Verreaux (1807–1873)

■ Barn Owl 35 cm | 14" ▶

The white owl. This owl appears longer-legged than most others and has a heart-shaped face with jet-black eyes. At night, listen out for its loud, screaming "*shriek*" call. Like most other owls, this enigmatic species is secretive and shy but it often roosts in buildings in towns and villages, emerging at dusk to feed on rats and other rodents. It is among the most cosmopolitan of all birds and is found on all the continents apart from Antarctica.

Unlike most other owls, the Barn Owl's middle claw is pectinate meaning that it has a serrated edge, often used for preening. Other bird families with pectinate claws include the nightjars and herons.

■ Square-tailed / Gabon Nightjar 23 cm | 9"

A highly camouflaged nocturnal bird of open woodland and bushy gardens. This species behaves in a similar manner to the Slender-tailed Nightjar and the two can be difficult to separate but this species shows a square-ended tail rather than a wedge-ended tail. The best identification feature is the call, which is a continuous low "*churr*" that is quite different from that of the Slender-tailed Nightjar. This bird can be easily found at Speke Bay where it roosts in the gardens of various lodges.

■ Slender-tailed Nightjar 25 cm | 10"

An amazingly camouflaged nocturnal bird of open acacia areas. Difficult to find on the ground, nightjars are easier to see as they rise to hawk for insects at dusk and dawn, sometimes coming to feed on moths at the lights of lodges and camps, when they look like a falcon or a large swift. This is the most abundant of the nightjar species that are resident in the Serengeti and NCA, and shows a long tail with an obvious wedge at the tip. At night, listen out for its monotonous call which is similar to a car alarm "*we-we-we-we-we…*"; in flight, its call is a squeaky "*wik-wik-ik*". A good local guide may know where to find one roosting on the ground during the day.

▼

☐ Blue-headed Coucal 46 cm | 18" ▼

A large and boldly marked bird of reedbeds and papyrus swamp. This huge member of the cuckoo family is only likely to be encountered on the edge of Lake Victoria, where it could only be confused with the White-browed Coucal (*page 120*) that also occurs here. However, the Blue-headed Coucal is larger and shows a completely dark cap and neck, which often looks black from a distance but shows a blue-sheen in good light. This contrasts with the off-white throat and breast that lacks any streaking. It can often be heard calling its series of very low "*woop*" notes, especially in the mornings.

Swamp Flycatcher 14 cm | 5"

A small, dumpy, brown bird with a white throat and belly. This friendly little flycatcher is not uncommon along the edge of Lake Victoria and often allows a close approach. Its shape is generally more round than other similar flycatchers, such as the African Grey Flycatcher (*page 172*), and it is the only one to show a broad brown breast-band. Young birds are similar but heavily spotted on the head and back.

▼

Black-headed Gonolek
21 cm | 8"

A stunning bushshrike of leafy gardens and overgrown woodland. Despite its glowingly bright plumage, this bird is a shy and retiring species that can be difficult to see well. Attention is often drawn to it by its distinctive song emanating from a thicket or bushy tree – a loud "*chee-oo chee-oo*" that is often followed by a grating "*chr-chr-chr*". Immature birds may only show a few crimson feathers on the underparts and instead have a heavily barred pattern from the throat to the belly.

▼

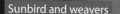

The nest of the Grosbeak Weaver is an elegant and tightly woven dome of fine fibres, usually built among tall reeds, that shows an obvious folded-back entrance hole at the side, .

Female

Taxonomists have determined that this weaver has no close relatives and may in fact not even be a weaver at all!

Male

Grosbeak Weaver 17 cm | 6¾"

A very large and chunky-billed dark-brown weaver of swamps and reedy margins. Identification is fairly straightforward as males are solid-looking birds with a white forehead and white flashes in the wing. Females are lighter brown and show extensive streaking on the underparts and a yellow base to the bill. They are highly gregarious and form substantial flocks in wetland areas, both on the lake shore and inland. It is often called the Thick-billed Weaver.

Red-chested Sunbird ▶

breeding male 14 cm | 5½"; female 11 cm | 4½"

An attractive sunbird with a green head and red breast-band. This species looks very similar to the Beautiful Sunbird (*page 154*), which it replaces on the shores of the lake, but is slightly bigger with a shorter tail. It may appear all-dark at a distance but in good light shows a vibrant red band on the breast above which is a band of purple, while the belly is matt black. Females are fairly nondescript but show soft mottling on the throat and breast, unlike the female Beautiful Sunbird which is plain below.

▪ Slender-billed Weaver 11 cm | 4½" ▼

A tiny yellow weaver with a slender bill. Pairs and small groups of this delightful little weaver can be found close to the edge of Lake Victoria, where it inhabits reedbeds, papyrus swamps and lodge gardens, often in association with other weavers. Males show a sharp-edged black mask while females have a bright-yellow head and black, beady eyes. In addition to reeds and sedges, birds can sometimes be seen feeding in thatched roofs, creeping like small yellow warblers rather than 'bouncing' like most typical weavers.

Male

Female

Male

Female

'Victoria Masked Weaver' male

Female

Male

Northern Brown-throated Weaver
14 cm | 5"

A distinctive yellow weaver with white eyes and a brownish face. Easily separated from the other weavers shown here, this species shows a dark-brown face in males and a rich, buffy face in females but the best identification feature is the pale eyes in both sexes. It is common along the edge of the Lake Victoria, where it nests in reedbeds and papyrus swamps.

Golden-backed Weaver 13 cm | 5"

A distinctive weaver with a black hood and neck and dark-chestnut underparts. A bright blaze of yellow on the back runs all the way down the rump. The bright-red eye can be difficult to observe against the black hood, although when seen this feature can be used to distinguish this species from Yellow-backed Weaver. Non-breeding males appear very tatty but often show the tell-tale signs of black against an otherwise yellowish head. Females are very similar to other female weavers on this page but show a dark eye and usually some yellow on the belly.

In the Speke Gulf and widely in Uganda, Northern Brown-throated Weavers frequently interbreed with Yellow-backed Weavers to create a hybrid known as 'Victoria Masked Weaver', which looks almost identical to the Northern Masked Weaver, a species that has its stronghold in Sudan.

☐ Yellow-backed Weaver 13 cm | 5"

An attractive weaver with a black hood and a yellow neck. Superficially similar to the Golden-backed Weaver (note the similarity between the names), this weaver also shows a chestnut breast but it is a brighter shade and typically turns to yellow on the belly. Rather than having a solid black hood, the Yellow-backed Weaver has a large yellow patch on the back of the neck that contrasts strongly with the black head, and has a green (not yellow) back. Females can be told from female Golden-backed Weavers by their white underparts.

Male

Female

The nest of the Golden-backed Weaver shows an obvious dome-shape, lacks an entrance tunnel and is always over water.

Male

Female

Often called Jackson's Golden-backed Weaver. See Jackson's Widowbird (*page 71*) for more about Sir Frederick Jackson.

Whiskered Tern 26 cm | 10"

A very attractive resident tern, the Whiskered Tern is easy to identify in the breeding season due to the combination of black cap, white cheeks and sooty-grey belly. It is less easy to identify in non-breeding plumage as it appears very similar to a non-breeding White-winged Black Tern. However, there are a few useful identification features, particularly the lack of an obvious black 'teardrop' behind the eye. Juveniles are surprisingly easy to identify as they are rusty-coloured on the back. Although sometimes found on lakes in the NCA and in the Serengeti, it is most common on Lake Victoria. Birds feed by making shallow dives for small fish but will also hawk over wet grass away from the lake in search of insects and larvae.

Breeding

White-winged Black Tern 23 cm | 9"

A stunning migrant tern that is very easy to separate from Whiskered Tern in breeding plumage but very difficult in non-breeding plumage. Perhaps the most helpful features are that White-winged Black Tern has a small and narrow black bill, very short red legs, a dark leading edge to the wing and often dark inner flight feathers and a few retained black feathers from the breeding plumage. It also shows a white rump and tail in all plumages that usually contrasts with the darker back. This species often gathers in big flocks and hawks over grass for insects and other invertebrates, and feeds far less on fish. It is only likely to be encountered between September and April. You may sometimes see this bird referred to as White-winged Tern but because many terns have white wings the traditional name is used here.

White-winged Black Terns
Non-breeding

Whiskered Tern

Breeding

Non-breeding

White-winged Black Tern

Breeding

Non-breeding

Grey-headed Gull

Breeding

Non-breeding

◻ **Grey-headed Gull** 40 cm | 16" ▼

The common small gull of Lake Victoria. Usually gathering in sizeable flocks, these pale, boisterous birds are equally happy scavenging their food as they are stealing it from herons and cormorants, a behaviour known as kleptoparasitism. The grey head is present when the bird is in breeding condition but otherwise it is white with black smudges behind the eyes. The less common Black-headed Gull (*not shown*) from Europe is smaller and paler.

Breeding

207

Great Cormorant

Reed Cormorant

☐ Reed Cormorant
53 cm | 21"
A dark, duck-sized bird of open waters. Considerably smaller than the Great Cormorant, this bird is also much smaller in its proportions, with the exception of having a comparatively longer tail (and hence is often referred to as Long-tailed Cormorant). Adults are dark-necked and immatures much paler, while breeding adults sport a short crest above the bill. Although less obvious than the Great Cormorant, this bird is common on Lake Victoria.

☐ Great Cormorant 100 cm | 40"
A pied goose-sized bird of open waters. There is great variation in the plumage of these thickset waterbirds: some adults are white-breasted whereas others are mostly black with a white chin. However, when in breeding plumage, all show a large white patch on the thigh. Immature birds are usually off-white on the entire underside. With the benefit of impressive webbed feet, they are excellent swimmers and their diet consists almost entirely of fish caught underwater. Various races of this species can be found across Africa, Asia, Europe, Australia and the eastern seaboard of North America.

In parts of the Far East, particularly in China, people use tethered cormorants to catch fish for their own consumption.

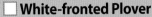

☐ Common Ringed Plover
20 cm | 8"

A squat, lake-shore wader with a single breast-band. This chunky little wader is a migrant from the north and is readily seen along the edges of lakes and marshes from September to April. It is easily told from similar African plovers by the single black band across the breast, a white collar at the back of the neck and short, orange-yellow legs. Immature birds are less well marked than adults.

▼

☐ White-fronted Plover
17 cm | 6½"

A pale wader of sandy Lake Victoria shores. Although seen regularly on sandy beaches on the coast, this smart little shorebird breeds in only very small numbers inland – and is one of the prize species that makes a birder's journey to Speke Bay so worthwhile. Breeding adults may show a black spot on top of the crown and the obvious white patch above the bill is present on adults and young. The face is whiter than similar small plovers that may occur, such as Kittlitz's (*page 31*) and Common Ringed Plovers that also show a black stripe through the eye.

▼

Adult

Immature

209

Further reading and useful resources

Suggested further reading

The Birds of East Africa by Terry Stevenson and John Fanshawe. Published in 2002 by Christopher Helm.

The Birds of Kenya and Northern Tanzania by Dale A. Zimmerman, Donald A. Turner, David J. Pearson, Doug Pratt and Ian Willis. 2nd Edition published in 2005 by Christopher Helm.

I highly recommend both of these outstanding books to anyone interested in taking their birding to the next level, and for East African explorations beyond the Serengeti.

Whose Bird? By Bo Beolens and Michael Watkins. Published in 2003 by Christopher Helm.

The anecdotes about the people that have birds named after them were gleaned from this book. It is a highly interesting read that I cannot recommend highly enough.

Birds of Africa: South of the Sahara by Ian Sinclair and Peter Ryan. 2nd Edition published in 2010 by C Struik.

The most comprehensive field guide to the birds of this incredible continent.

Online resources

www.tanzaniabirdatlas.com

This fantastic project requires YOUR Tanzanian bird records. By collecting data on a monthly basis and concentrating on evidence of breeding, the project hopes to understand much more about the seasonality of Tanzanian birdlife. There's a friendly community of birders online to help identify bird images, offer advice and the occasional birding trip out too. Be part of it!

www.serengeti.org
The official website of the Serengeti National Park.

www.ngorongorocrater.org
The official website of the Ngorongoro Conservation Area.

www.tanzaniaparks.com
The official website of Tanzania National Parks (TANAPA).

www.disabledbirdersassociation.co.uk
A fantastic resource that seeks to improve access for people with disabilities to reserves, facilities and services for birding.

www.fatbirder.com
You don't have to be overweight to enjoy this web resource about birds and birding for birders!

www.serengetinationalpark.com

For unbiased, informative, accurate and up to date information on all things relating to the Serengeti National Park, especially accommodation.

www.tusk.org

Get involved with the organisation that is "Protecting Wildlife, Supporting Communities, Promoting Education" in Africa.

For anyone seeking further inspiration about the joys of safari in Northern Tanzania, check out these wonderful blogs by two of the most experienced safari guides working in the region.

www.privileged-observer.blogspot.co.uk by Richard Knocker.

www.ethan-kinsey.blogspot.co.uk by Ethan Kinsey.

Acknowledgements

Such a book would not be possible without the help of many people so I would like to take this opportunity to thank those who have given me generous assistance along the way.

First and foremost, I would like thank my wife Vicki for so many things but most of all for being my wife, always looking out for me and keeping me on right side of normal (well, most of the time). Secondly, I would like to thank Neil and Liz Baker for their help since I began birding in Tanzania in 2008. Not only have they had an answer to my numerous odd questions but I would like to 'tip my hat' in recognition for all their hard work on the Tanzania Bird Atlas project which is managed by them both. Thanks for leading the way in promoting a greater understanding of birds to all in Tanzania and beyond. Email them on tzbirdatlas@yahoo.co.uk.

For their friendship and unwavering support at all times, thanks go to dear friends Tony and Betty Archer, Dudu (Deborah) Beaton, Lulu Keeble and Graham Roy, Ken and Michelle Dyball, Nigel Archer (Nigel Archer Safaris) and Mike Cheffings (Bateleur Safaris). For their warm hospitality and taking the very best care of us when on safari, we would also like to thank the following: Chris and Nani Schmeling at Kisima Ngeda - Lake Eyasi, Peter Kerr and team at Gibb's Farm, Jan Halfwerk and Gert Borst at Speke Bay Lodge. A special mention also to the team at Asilia Africa for their kindness and support during our visits to Dunia Camp and Oliver's Camp (Tarangire National Park) which we thoroughly enjoyed. Wisdom and friendship also came from James Robertson (Ker & Downey), Joe du Plessis (Asilia Africa), Niall Anderson (&Beyond), Richard Knocker (Nomad), and Clint Schipper (Kuro Expeditions), for which I am indebted.

Finally, to the team at **WILD**Guides: Rob Still, Andy and Gill Swash and Brian Clews (designer and editors and proof-readers extraordinaire) – you have once again weaved your magic to create something quite beautiful. Thanks again for your hard work and diligence in bringing the Birds of the Serengeti to life for me.

Photographic credits

All the images included in this book were taken by the author, Adam Scott Kennedy, with the exception of the following:

Gert Borst (spekebay.com): Lake Victoria marsh (*page 21*).

Greg & Yvonne Dean (WorldWildlifeImages.com): Common Kestrel, male and female perched (*page 57*); Giant Kingfisher (*page 100*); Black-crowned Tchagra (*page 142*); Red-faced Crombec (*page 149*); Golden-breasted Bunting (*page 165*); Streaky Seedeater (*page 185*); Banded Martin, perched (*page 187*); Eurasian Bee-eater, perched (*page 194*); White-throated Bee-eater, perched (*page 194*); Pearl-spotted Owlet (*page 196*); Verreaux's Eagle Owl (*page 197*); Common Ringed Plover, adult (*page 209*).

Vicki Kennedy: Ostrich chicks, (*page 25*); Martial Eagle (*page 44*); Woodland Kingfisher (*page 125*); Spotted Morning Thrush (*page 144*).

Paul Oliver (paul-oliver.com): Maasai village (*page 17*).

Andy & Gill Swash (WorldWildlifeImages.com): NCA scenery (*pages 12–13*); Lake Magadi (*page 14*); Pied Kingfisher (*page 14*); Fischer's Lovebirds (*page 15*); Ndutu Safari Lodge (*Page 15*); Variable Sunbird (*page 15*); Silverbird (*page 16*); White-winged Black Tern (*page 21*); Double-banded Courser (*page 31*); Chestnut-bellied Sandgrouse (*page 34*); Egyptian Vulture in flight (*page 43*); Bateleur (*page 47*); Pallid Harrier, immature female in flight (*page 52*); Montagu's Harrier, female in flight (*page 52*); Lesser Kestrel, male perched and male and female in flight (*pages 56–57*); Eurasian Roller, perched and in flight (*page 59*); Northern Wheatear, male and female (*page 66*); Capped Wheatear (*page 67*); Pied Wheatear, male and female (*page 67*); Grassland Pipit (*page 69*); Ruff, female and immature (*page 95*); Yellow Wagtail – 'Blue-headed', 'Syke's' and 'Yellow-headed' (*page 102*); Long-crested Eagle, in flight (*page 105*); Grey-breasted Spurfowl (*page 109*); Diederik Cuckoo (*page 122*); Usambiro Barbet, both images (*page 128*); Northern White-crowned Shrike (*page 138*); Rattling Cisticola (*page 148*); Beautiful Sunbird, male and female (*page 154*); African Stonechat, female (*page 185*); Eurasian Bee-eater, in flight (*page 195*); Whiskered Tern, breeding in flight (*page 207*); White-winged Black Tern, breeding, in flight (*page 207*).

Roger Tidman: Montagu's Harrier, male in flight from above (*page 52*).

Kori Bustard

Scientific names of the bird species included in this book

Most of the guides working in the Serengeti and NCA use English names when referring to the birds they see. However, given the diversity of countries from which visitors to the region come, these names may not be familiar to all. Some visitors will, however, know birds by their universally accepted scientific name. The following list therefore includes all the birds mentioned in this book, ordered alphabetically by their scientific name. It is cross-referenced to the English name(s) used and the page number(s) on which the bird appears. English names are highlighted in **bold** for those species that are illustrated. For ease of reference, the page number for the main account for each species is shown in **bold**; other places in the book where a photograph appears are shown in *italics*. The other species mentioned in the book that are not illustrated are shown in normal text.

Index

Names in **bold** highlight the species that are afforded a full account.
Bold numbers indicate the page number of the main species account.
Bold blue numbers relate to other page(s) on which a photograph appears.
Normal black numbers are used to indicate the page(s) where the species is mentioned, but not illustrated. For scientific names, see *page 211*.